BEFORE I LEAVE YOU

Before I Leave You

A MEMOIR ON SUICIDE, ADDICTION AND HEALING

ROBERT IMBEAULT

HOUNDSTOOTH
PRESS

BEFORE I LEAVE YOU

A Memoir on Suicide, Addiction and Healing

ISBN 978-1-5445-0659-3 *Hardcover*

      978-1-5445-0658-6 *Paperback*

      978-1-5445-0657-9 *Ebook*

      978-1-5445-0677-7 *Audiobook*

For my wife, Elmira,
and our daughters,
Vivian and Willow

Contents

Passwords

I WONDER IF AN EMAIL CAN BE SENT ON A TIME DELAY. You compose it, set the day and time you'd like it to be sent, and it sends at that time. Has this been invented? I'm sure it has. I need to do this with my passwords.

Okay, I'm having a bad night. That's all it is. My therapist said that I should try to identify what catastrophic thoughts are going through my head on nights like these. She repeatedly used the word "catastrophic" when describing these thoughts. I suppose the word is suitable when describing the thoughts of a person who no longer wants to live, which is how I'm feeling tonight.

I walk over to my closet and grab a tie. I don't wear ties anymore. Their primary use had been to play with Logan, my constantly purring, white Persian cat. Logan loves to bat his paws at them while I dangled it in his face. The tie I picked was knotted already from the other half-ass attempts, but now it's go-time. It's a strange, surprisingly comfortable decision. I wrap the tie around my neck while sitting down on my staircase, then secure the other end to an upper railing. I can barely lean forward without the tie tightening. I know if I just sit here and relax long enough, the blood flow to my brain will stop and I'll pass out. Gravity would do the rest. It's like the autoerotic asphyxiation stories I've seen on TV cop dramas. A man masturbates while slouching forward with his neck tied similar to how I described above, but takes too long and ends up dead. I never thought to masturbate while doing this, but it's probably not a good idea given how I'd be found. I wonder what Kevin would say to me if he was around. He's been the one constant in my life since I was a kid. I'm pretty sure he'd be pissed.

I pass out slowly, and right on cue, the room goes black. I let go and for a few seconds I'm at peace. A blissful nothing. Tension dissolves into the ether and my body falls. The fall forward jerks me awake. The noose tightens from the fall and I can't breathe. The room is still dark to my eyes and I can barely lift my hands. I try to scream but can't—I have no breath to do it. I'm deaf now, only able to hear the tapping sounds of my hands and feet as I struggle. It's as if my head is underwater. Somehow, I focus enough to loosen the knot and stumble down the remaining stairs. I struggle to breathe through my crushed windpipe. Bile makes its way out and onto the floor. I lay quietly gaining consciousness while contemplating this embarrassing failure. I am now either one of those this-is-a-cry-for-attention losers, or just plain incompetent. I hate myself even more. I consider that maybe I want to live for something, but am more convinced that a natural survival instinct kicked in. Logan sits there watching. I wonder what he was thinking. He's probably excited to see the tie.

I hadn't thought about the list before this attempt. The list of things to do to prepare for being dead, I mean. The passwords that the ex-wife or friends get so they have access to my laptops, phones, and email so they can continue as if nothing happened. To make sure the banking information gets to the ex in case she needs to transfer some money since I wouldn't be doing it anymore. And this might seem a bit silly for most; to wrap up all the significant work-related projects. It was a company that I started nine years earlier and there was always work to be done. I had a young partner, Mitchel, and I didn't want him inconvenienced, other than losing a close friend and partner to suicide. I wanted the people I left behind to have a smooth transition. I'd describe these thoughts as considerate, not catastrophic.

I wasn't always like this. I didn't always want to die. I've done and seen extraordinary things in my life both wonderful and terrible. I've lived homeless on the street, built successful businesses, met the Queen of England, and swam with Great White Sharks. I've hurt too many people to count; I've lied, I've cheated, and was arrested on more than one occasion. The protagonist in any story is a champion of a cause or idea. A hero. Something I am not. I am someone who barely hung on. The following is the story of how I struggled to survive childhood to build a beautiful life only to annihilate it in a self-indulgent, self-destructing cavorting dance with drugs and alcohol, leaving heartbreak and pain in my wake. I am not the hero. I am the one who stared death in the face and taunted it. This story is about giving up. This story is about holding on.

Spiderman

SIX YEARS BEFORE MY CATASTROPHIC TIE AFFAIR, I WAS alone. Electing to spend most of my time at work only to go home to an empty condo. Empty except for Spring, my affectionate, dark-grey, Maine Coon cat. Spring was a kitten when I started my first business, 10Count, about five years earlier. 10Count was a software company which was doing well at the expense of my social life. My nights were spent eating dinner on my light beige leather sofa in front of an open laptop while Spring sat perched beside me hoping that I'd share some food. I didn't have cable television, which meant I missed the final months of the US election debates between Barrack Obama and John McCain—something I may have wanted to witness. Instead, I chose to play DVD box sets of series like *24*, *Buffy the Vampire Slayer*, and *Angel*. The episodes served as a comforting backdrop filled with anxiety and drama. Sounds as familiar to me as the white noise of crashing ocean waves. The flat screen TV, a new technology at the time, was mounted on a bare white wall with all its wires neatly unseen. There's something about cables and wires not being tucked away that bothered me. If you're alone for long enough, seemingly unimportant details become unsettling itches.

I rarely had anyone over, but my condo was spotless. I washed the dishes after I used them, swept the dark wood floors daily to keep the cat-hair at bay, and laundry would never accumulate to more than one load. When I brought back the crisp Armani dress shirts from the dry cleaner, I ritualized the process of removing each one from its plastic cover, then replaced the wire hanger the shirt was on with a polished wooden one. When I was done, I would ensure each hanger was two-finger widths apart and grouped the clothing together by color. I returned the wire hangers to the dry cleaner on my next visit. When I realized that these seemingly harmless rituals were beginning to consume me, I felt I needed to meet someone. There was no need to tell Kevin. He was leaving me alone for the most part anyway. I was safe in the bubble I had created so there was no need for him to reach out.

A dating site, I thought, was an acceptable way to meet someone without humiliating myself by asking someone I knew for a set-up, which would be admitting I was desperate and lonely. It also meant I could bypass acting social in a crowd, an undertaking that pressed my stomach into a panic from mere consideration. Online dating seemed to me to be efficient although it was challenging to take it seriously. Anyone can describe themselves in any way they want to in their profile, so I created a profile of jokes. Other than my age, thirty-two at the time, the answers I provided to the profile questions were the exact opposite of what I felt potential mates would want to hear. It went something like this: "I live at home with my parents, do not own my own business, not a fan of laughing or doing anything outside of the house. I love playing video games and not paying attention to people when they speak, and if you're looking for encouragement or support, you won't find it here." I was banking on someone finding it at least mildly funny and, who knows, maybe there were some connections I'd make to fill the lonely nights. Instead, I got hate mail. A lot of it. And I read them all. Some of the responses took my answers seriously and abhorred Bizzaro me. Others felt I was mocking everyone on the site, including my lonely compatriots.

A few weeks had passed when I noticed that a woman with the handle Trixycat had viewed my profile. I said "Hi." A few days went by until she replied. The photo in her profile revealed that she was pretty, blonde, and was looking up at the camera. The right side of her upper lip was subtly higher, making her smile endearingly crooked. Her name was Perrine, and after a few days of graceless messaging through the dating site, we decided to meet in person at a restaurant in the city for a drink.

It's a strange thing to arrange your own blind date. Could this be considered a blind date? It was someone

I'd never met in person although we were able to vet each other, mitigating the possibility of instant dislike followed by an awkward dismissal. Perrine had already cleared the first round of consideration. Was she a non-smoker? Check. Did she speak intelligently? Check. Was she kind? Check. That's all I needed to move on to the next phase. This may seem like I knew what I was doing. I did not. I walked into the nearly empty restaurant and noticed Perrine sitting at a table on the outside patio. I was surprised to see her out there on such a chilly night. Perrine smiled as I approached her. She was gorgeous in person.

"You're not five-ten," she said. She was right. I'm five-eight. Her eyes looked at me suspiciously. I had deliberately exaggerated on my profile, but in my defense, everything else was a lie also.

"I was rounding up," I answered with a smirk. To my relief, Perrine laughed with her crooked smile I remembered from her profile photo. I liked it immediately. It made her unique, special. I sat down, facing her, then blurted out, "To get the rest out in the open, I'm going through a divorce, and I don't want to get married again or have kids." Perrine studied my eyes as she registered my outburst. My breath shallowed. I felt my face warm. I looked around in silence. The restaurant was new but sat in the parking lot of an aging strip mall. The patio pushed its way into the lot, forfeiting a row of parking spots. As cars drove in, their lights shined on us like theatre spotlights.

"Umm, we just met," she stated in kind sarcasm. My hands trembled under the table, but I was glad to have spoken the words out loud. I couldn't be too careful.

"True, I just wanted to be as honest as I can."

Perrine nodded. The rest of the conversation was light and friendly. Perrine didn't hold my clodhopping proclamation nor my height against me. She admitted she was also a child of divorce and hesitant on marriage too. Agreeing that this wasn't a date, but rather a "meeting," we ended the night assuming that our relationship would reside within the lines of friendship.

We were wrong. We fell in love. Perrine worked as a counselor with mentally disabled adults. She also worked part-time for a family with two teenage boys who suffered from Muscular Dystrophy Duchene. I joined her at her part-time job, getting to know the family for a short while. Witnessing for the first time how Perrine interacted with the boys deepened my love and respect for her.

Within six months I asked Perrine to marry me. I knew she was "the one," a cliché we would repeat to our family and friends much to their disdain. We didn't care. We married the following summer at Perrine's grandparents' home, a beautiful cottage on a picturesque lake a few hours from our home in Ottawa. My younger sister, Michelle, acted as best man for the ceremony after which the groomsmen decided it would be a grand idea to go tubing in their tuxedos. Tubing is a sport where a boat drags people on an inflated tube at high speeds while the rider holds on for as long as they can handle. The wedding antics were worthy of a Norman Rockwell painting. Not too long after the wedding, we bought a house in the suburbs.

Perrine enjoyed being social with her friends and began bringing me along. Given that I'd spent most of my non-working time at home with little human socialization I was apprehensive but became more amiable over time. Perrine joked with her friends about how dating me was taking on a project, not unlike her mentally disabled clients at which they all seemed to chuckle. I was her "bird with a broken wing" and she promised to "fix" me.

While continuing to build my first company and starting a new one with two new partners, I encouraged Perrine to pursue interior design, for which she had a budding passion and talent. Taking my advice, she enrolled herself in courses and eventually began taking on clients. Our lives were happy and content. I had everything—a beautiful wife, a big house, and a fancy sports car. All the things I grew up believing would bring me happiness. We were living our happily-ever-after, and it was absolute bliss on paper. Until it wasn't.

* * *

For as long as I can remember I've had a fear of Spiderman. Seeing him on screen and in comic books frightened me. It was how I felt the Boogieman would look if he was real and, for most of my life, I believed he was. I met him. I was eight years old living with my mother in a dilapidated apartment building on Barton Street in Hamilton. One night I woke up to a silhouette of a man, almost like a shadow, standing in a dark corner of my bedroom. He was looking at me. I gasped in white cold terror. The figure shushed me and said, "Go back to sleep." I followed his instructions and fell back asleep. The memory of that night persisted throughout my life, often wondering if I dreamt it. The memory is different now. It has gone abruptly from a pixelated video clip to a high-definition, full-length motion picture.

I was in bed with Perrine reading. We often read in bed before falling asleep. We'd been married for three years and I was absorbed in the book, *God is Not Great* by Christopher Hitchens. A passage in the book described how a woman was sentenced to be stoned to death. Her crime was waiting in a car for her husband and speaking with another man without her husband or father present, a clear violation of Islamic law. The stoning was described in great detail. I thought to myself "How could they?" as I visualized the stoning, trying to understand how people could be so evil and cruel. Setting the book down on my lap, I turned to Perrine.

"How could someone be so cruel?" I asked. Then I added without thinking, "*And to a little boy?*"

Instantly, I was somewhere else. I couldn't turn away. I couldn't stop the projection in the theatre of my mind.

I was captive, paralyzed, and unable to look away from the film behind my eyelids. After the Boogieman's voice told me to go back to sleep, I turned around. I felt a hand on the back of my head as it forced it violently into the pillow. I didn't struggle. I was frozen with fear. I remember cringing at the pain and cowering until it was over. I'm not sure how long I lay there, but I didn't move when it ended. I heard him leave and I curled up. When there was enough light to assure me that I was alone, I collected the blood-soaked sheets and underwear for fear my mother would find them. I took them to the garbage chute and threw them away. I washed myself off and it was over. My mother woke up hung-over from another night out and I saw her vomit into the garbage can in the kitchen. She noticed nothing. It was just another shitty morning.

Still sitting next to Perrine, I replayed the scene over and over. Delirious, I fell off the bed. I made my way to the washroom where I evacuated the contents of my stomach. I embraced the bowl. I could feel Perrine's presence, but her voice sounded miles away. The outside world became an unfamiliar landscape. I was foreign to the world I was only visiting until now. My body lay in that world, on the bathroom floor, sobbing. Perrine sat close beside me, trying to comfort me. I'm not sure how much I was able to tell her, but she stayed. I lay catatonic at the base of the toilet bowl until Perrine brought me back to bed. I curled up and fell asleep just as that eight-year-old boy had done thirty years earlier.

My inability to fathom how someone could have raped an innocent little boy spun me into an endless loop of disbelief and confusion. My mind tried to understand it over and over, each time with no answer, each time carving away a piece of my sanity. Bewilderment rooted into every waking thought. I sunk into introversion, becoming painfully quiet. I refused to have sex with Perrine and resented her for not understanding. I refused to go to therapy or discuss it with anyone. It was the beginning of the end of my marriage with Perrine. I decided to distance myself from her so that I could crawl somewhere alone to die like an old, sick cat.

"This isn't working," I said, my eyes fixated on our glass coffee table. Perrine was already crying. We sat with space between us on an oversized sofa in the living room we had just renovated. Through the glass tabletop I could make out the reflection of the television on the refinished oak floors. It didn't shine as much during the day, but there was no light coming in this late at night. Perrine muted the television. Her teary eyes glared at me. Within my motionless body, my stomach protested with volcanic bursts of bile. It knew what I was about to do.

"You're not even trying to get better," she said. "You just sit there. You don't talk to a therapist or me. You clearly need help"

Still staring at the glass coffee table, I offered no counter. Tears slid down my face.

"Exactly," she snipped. Perrine took a deep breath to

gain composure. Her hand gently reached out to mine. She caressed my hand, inspecting the lifelines in my palm until her eyes met mine. "Are you absolutely positive that there is no way we can work this out? I'm willing to put in the work if you are."

Perrine was a no-nonsense person. She understood and lived her values and didn't want to be around anyone who didn't know and live theirs. Among her principles was her "open door policy." Perrine did not want to be with someone who didn't reciprocate one hundred percent. If her mate was even a little bit unsure, then he should leave and figure it out. She held herself accountable to the same rule. "If one of us isn't sure about the other, then it's not fair to either of us. I wouldn't chase you or beg you to come back if we broke up. I'm worth more than that. I'm worthy of being loved by someone completely." No nonsense.

"I don't know," I answered Perrine finally. We wept without comforting each other. Perrine walked out of the room. Her hands covered most of her face as she tried to hold back her tears. I felt Kevin watching me from across the room, but I didn't look up. I stayed on the oversized sofa numb to everything external. I begged for death to sweep in and take me. I wasn't looking for answers; I only wanted the questions to stop.

Descent

AT HOME, PERRINE AND I BARELY SPOKE. I WENT TO WORK in a dazed confusion hoping it would distract me from thinking about my life. Perrine did the same with her work. Weeks went by. Nothing changed. I needed something more to distract me from the constant re-reflection of my rape and subsequently losing Perrine.

I'd never been to Las Vegas. I had little interest in going to the American Southwest at all other than a passing interest in seeing the Grand Canyon. The interest in the Grand Canyon was born after seeing the movie with the same name in the Eighties starring Danny Glover and Kevin Klein. There wouldn't be time to see the Grand Canyon on this trip, however. I was invited to a bachelor party. I introduced the couple that was getting married, and the groom-to-be insisted I attend. Although celebrating love whilst in the depths of my questioning its very existence may have been hypocritical, I felt obligated to attend. I told no one about what was happening with

Perrine. Instead, I treated this trip as an escape from the turmoil of my inner hell.

The bachelor party was made up of the groom's friends and cousins, but one of them stood out—Mike Chowen. We only ever called him Chowen. Chowen was tall, thin and wore a fedora which he somehow made work. He wore embroidery decorated designer jeans and a colorful, paisley dress shirt. His crisp white collar and cuffs folded loosely over his forearms revealing colorful tattoos. He didn't smile but looked into my eyes when he spoke to me. Despite his thin frame, his voice held weight. It wasn't necessarily deep. Rather, it was articulate and clear. This surprised me given what he was wearing. I'd made a snap-judgment about Chowen, but soon learned that this book was very different from what I chose to see on the cover. Chowen was going through a break up of his own after a long relationship and was looking to dive into the depths of alcohol just like I was. I found someone lost like I was, which made me hopeful I wouldn't feel alone throughout the trip.

To the group, Chowen was the "Vegas Veteran." He had all the connections for clubs, girls, and drugs. The first club we entered was called Rain at the Palms Casino Resort. Chowen assured us that we would get a good booth and solid service. I had no idea what getting a good booth and solid service meant, but trusted that I was in good hands.

After some haggling, we followed Chowen through a

door and down a short narrow hallway. We passed other people in lines who watched as we walked ahead of them. The air was cool like it was everywhere else indoors in Vegas, and although we walked through clouds of smoke I could barely smell the stink of cigarettes. The further we trekked into the hallway, the harsher the bass thumped through my chest. The corridor opened to reveal hundreds, maybe thousands, of fists pumping in unison with the pulse of the music. Walking into Rain Nightclub, I felt as if I was walking into a new world and leaving my old one behind.

In a way, I was. The circular, gymnasium-size dancefloor was packed with dancers. They faced the DJ who stood on a stage behind a mountain of silver and black equipment cases. A metal chandelier the size of a car hung over the crowd, occasionally spewing fireballs. The bursts of heat warmed my skin. The poster at the entrance reading "The Hottest Club in Vegas" now made sense. Private booths crammed with well-dressed clubbers wrapped around the center of the club. The booths resembled office cubicles. Cubicles filled with groups of men sporting barely-buttoned dress shirts and women with big hair and tight dresses. Balcony booths on two additional floors overlooked the action. Ours was on the third floor.

I'd never experienced or understood why we nee͏ strategy for what's called "bottle service." W͏ of men went clubbing without bringi͏ they couldn't simply buy drinks as so many movies from the Eighties might suggest. They had to buy bottles of liquor or champagne. Bottle service catapults you from the hundreds of dollars you budgeted to spend on the already extortionately priced drinks to the thousands. If you did the math, however, it was less expensive than buying the same number of drinks one by one. However, the math didn't make the idea of spending thousands of dollars on booze any more palatable. Next comes the placement of the booth, which is correlated with the amount of money you're willing to spend. If you were okay with being in the back far from the dance floor and/or DJ, you could get by with a lower minimum. But if you wanted to be in the action, where the girls are, you have to pay more. Sometimes much more.

There is a hack to get these superior booths, which is to tip the host heavily. It's called a "handshake" as a patron folded cash to fit in his palm to discreetly pass him the money in a handshake motion. A handshake in the hundreds could save you thousands in the right circumstances. On our first night, we were in the back. The men in the bachelor party were not in the habit of spending and were in it for the savings rather than the cachet.

As this was a bachelor party, there was a requirement for women to join the party. There was no shortage of women at the club. Enter "bottle rats." A bottle rat is a derogatory term for men or women who infiltrate a booth by flirting or simply just walking in and helping themselves to a group's paid-for bottles of liquor. In general, this can be a mutually beneficial transaction. Men want to flirt with beautiful women, and the women want to drink free alcohol. Sometimes, however, it's not so clear cut. Some women flirt their way into a booth and get drinks for their other friends or boyfriends. Others are merely rude and presumptuous. Removing said offenders from the booth can be both awkward and challenging. Many groups ask a bouncer to escort them out which invariably leads to watching as a large man makes his way over to the transgressor in question, taps them on the shoulder and points to the booth's exit. The requesting patron invariably looks away to avoid any unpleasant eye contact. Some wrongdoers leave quietly, others make a scene. That first night, a few bottle rats were asked to leave, but they left with simple scowls.

Although the music didn't offend me and the guys were friendly, I was painfully uncomfortable. I was surrounded by thousands of people having what seemed to be the time of their lives while I sat in an upper dark corner, behind most of the group, completely alone. The deafening clamor of the music and crowd made a simple conversation strenuous and annoying. When any of the guys tried to talk to me, I pointed to my ears indicating I couldn't understand them even though most of the time I could. I held my prop, the rum and Diet Coke I wasn't drinking, and nodded my head to the music as if I were enjoying myself. I stared blankly out into the crowd while all I could think about was Perrine.

Rick, a member of our group, interrupted my stupor by bumping his shoulder into mine to show me the vial of cocaine held between his thumb and finger and an expression that asked if I wanted some. I politely declined and almost as soon as I did, he asked if I wanted Ecstasy. The question suddenly, violently transported me back in time. The music was gone; the people weren't moving. The memory of the first time I tried Ecstasy five years earlier consumed me.

For most of my late twenties and into my thirties, I was vehemently against any kind of drug, including alcohol. I tried not to judge but certainly did. I shook my head at drunks, potheads, coke-heads, and I was never around meth-heads. When I met Perrine, I was already in my thirties, and I had fallen so hard for her that I trusted her deeply. My drug knowledge was limited to persistent and persuasive commercials from the Eighties. Nancy Reagan's "Just Say No" campaign and the "This is your brain on drugs" ads showing an egg frying on a cast iron pan. I heard from a television show that taking Ecstasy was like taking an ice cream scoop to your brain and that it drained your spinal fluid. I have since learned these claims were all bullshit spread to scare teenagers and they succeeded. You won that round, Nancy. Perrine shared her experiences with the drug highlighting how great the sex was. We decided to try it together.

Perrine and I "scored some X," an expression I felt too uncomfortable to use out loud, and scheduled a night to "drop" and another day afterward to recover. After I swallowed the pill my skin quivered in fear while I asked myself, "What the fuck did I just do?" The unanswered question faded with alcoholic distraction. We closed our eyes as we danced to music, hoping our anticipation would soon be replaced by our high. An hour went by, and nothing. Another hour went by and still nothing. We hadn't scored X; we procured duds. I felt simultaneously disappointed and relieved, but realized I'd overcome my apprehension and was now even more curious to try it. We scored some more X a few weeks later and tried again.

The pill looked suspiciously like the duds from our first non-experience, which set my expectations low. We toasted our drinks and downed the new pills. An hour went by and nothing happened. I considered the idea that I was one of those people who was impervious to these drugs. Do those people exist? Frustrated, possibly a little drunk, I popped another pill. Perrine's eyes widened and she cried, "Wait! It just might take longer!" It was too late. The second pill was gone. She laughingly and worryingly shook her head.

We stumbled our way into bed. As we were kissing, a heated tingling made its way from the tip of my toes to my knees to my waist to my spine to my scalp. My body turned into a pulsating blob of jelly. Every crevice of every ripple of Perrine's lips slid against mine. My hands felt like they were microscopic conduits able to sense every intention of her pores. I stretched from my toes to my temples, contracting every atom of my being. Overwhelming joy washed over me. Filled with pleasure, I hovered above the bed like a speck of dust caught in sunlight. I tried to speak but forgot how. I was okay with it. I remember trying to say how incredible I felt and struggled to get it out. I was fully conscious and as high as fuck. I loved everything. I loved Perrine. I loved my cat. I loved the buttons on my shirts and the lint in my pockets. Kevin didn't exist and all was right in the world. Walking presented a challenge at first. It was as if I was walking in warm, caressing water and my legs were made of air-filled pool floaties.

After a few more drinks, I wanted to see what sex was going to be like, but I was distracted by how gloriously soft my cat, Spring, was and I decided to pet him. Spring purred loudly. Eventually, Perrine had to come to find me as I had apparently been petting him for forty-five minutes. Sex was the last thing on my mind, but even if it was, I was ill prepared. It was as though I'd brought warm gum to a gunfight. But it didn't matter. I was high for the first time in my life. I wanted to enjoy it, not be brought down by the consistently overwhelming pressure of sexual performance.

Hours vanished, and the sun started to rise. Perrine warned me about the perils of the comedown, but I wasn't prepared for what was about to happen. I curled up on the couch and my body, in exhausted combustion, started to convulse. Every muscle contracted and relaxed in unison. No longer able to discern which way was up, I held on to

Perrine tightly. My head rested in her lap as she stroked my hair while a buzzing drone rumbled in my ears. Simultaneously exhausted and completely awake, I lay there for what felt like hours until I was able to fall asleep. Sixteen hours later my eyes opened. My body felt like it had boxed a hundred rounds then ran a marathon for good measure. I could barely get out of bed let alone get into a car and drive. Our planned one-day recovery became three, and I returned to work on Tuesday. The undeniable exhaustion made for challenging conference calls and, worse, in-person meetings. Weeks after the soiree into Ecstasy, my body began to feel normal and, though I enjoyed the experience of being high, I vowed never to do it again.

"We can split it if you want," Rick suggested. The music thumped in my chest as if to say *do it, do it, do it.*

"Sure," I heard myself answer. Rick looked around inconspicuously then examined the pill and bit it. I watched intently as he placed the remaining portion into my palm.

"This stuff is so fucking good!" Rick shouted over the music. I slammed my palm over my mouth and washed it down with my rum and Diet Coke. Instantly, I panicked, but just as quickly began to justify what I'd just done to myself. I had nothing to lose and I wanted the weight of my imploding marriage and life off my shoulders. I nodded a thank you to Rick and he put his arm around me. We toasted our glasses and bounced our heads to the base. A few drinks, later my wish was granted. I started to drift away. I stomped my foot to confirm I was still firmly on the ground. The exercise almost tipped me over. If I tried to spit, only dry air would appear. I leaned on the couch. Chowen came to my side.

"This your first time doing X?" I answered in a language possible decipherable by whales. Chowen placed a water bottle into my hand and said he'd make sure I kept drinking water tonight. Cleverly, he asked me to ensure he did the same. I wasn't sure if giving me that responsibility was a ploy to ensure I drank my own water, or if he seriously wanted me to make sure he'd be OK. Either way, the two of us were on the water train. My mind was clear, but my skin mimicked an electric blanket set to max. Absurdly happy, I felt connected with everyone around me. I was no longer off in the corner by myself and I drank whatever was handed to me.

Like five years earlier, it felt as though sympathetic, loving hands were massaging every muscle, like fingertips were gently gliding all over my body. At the height of the wave, the music thread itself into my pores, penetrating into my temporal lobe. Excited screams emanated from the crowd. It was a song I had never heard before; "Levels" by Avicii. Its melodic symphony played the exact notes that summoned the greatest joy I could ever imagine. I was floating over the crowd. When I found my footing, I was a different person. I talked to everyone around me, even people who weren't a part of the bachelor party. I was social. I was fearless. Kevin would not have approved, but he wasn't there so I pushed him out of my mind.

As the night unfolded, I took another half pill. When the club closed, the guys excitedly called a limo-bus to pick us up. This surprised me given the thrifty nature of our club endeavor, but again that was my naiveté. In order to get a group of men to a world-renowned strip club, the savvy club offered a free limo-bus to come and collect them. Before I knew it, I was on my way to the Spearmint Rhino. Of course, another half of Ecstasy would only amplify the night's enjoyment so I partook. Another aversion of mine was strip clubs. My struggle with them wasn't sanctimonious but rather multi-level psychological discomforts. I could not reconcile the sexless sexuality with the awkward, sobering exchange of money; teasing real human connection for money was a torment I felt no desire to subject myself to. But tonight was a different night. Tonight, the drugs were in charge.

Chowen continued my education at Vegas University. The same deal to get a good seat or table at the strip club would involve another "handshake" tip. The same bottle service rule applies in these establishments as well but to a much more affordable pricing structure.

The inside of the Spearmint Rhino was larger than I expected. It was darker than the Rain nightclub, but I could make out dozens of tables scattered between three stages. Each stage showcased its own dancer holding on to its invariable pole and surrounded by seats set closely against the stage, affectionately known as "perverts row." There were plenty of smokers throughout, but like the rest of Vegas, the smoke was filtered out effectively.

"It smells like coconuts," I said to Chowen, each of us chuckling.

"That's the skin cream the dancers use."

We procured ourselves a table and as soon as we sat down, were swarmed. Dancers—they do not like the term "stripper"—approached us and maneuvered in with great agility and finesse landing on our laps, wrapping one arm around our neck. The dancers wore lingerie and their coconut skin cream made them feel especially soft when combined with my Ecstasy-assisted senses.

"Wow, you guys are having fun tonight. Where are y'all from?" a dancer asked. Any answer returned a, "Wow, tell me more." We loved it nonetheless. Chowen politely asked the dancers to give us a few minutes, and the first wave of ladies left.

"Okay, what's the plan?" asked Chowen. I had no idea what I was doing, so I shrugged, which made him laugh.

"How does this work?" I asked, shooting back my first unreasonably priced rum and Diet Coke. Chowen motioned to another dancer to wait while we spoke. The music changed from a rock-and-roll song to country and I saw a tall, curvy brunette step on stage wearing a sequined cowboy hat. Chowen watched her as he explained.

"So, you can buy dances which are three songs for

twenty dollars, or you can go to the VIP room where you can get more intimate, but it costs much more."

"You mean it's a brothel?"

"There's no sex, just more touching," Chowen explained. "But there is a chance you can pick one up and meet her later." I wasn't there to pick anyone up. I just wanted to be high with my new friends.

"Ah, OK. I'm good out here with you guys." I didn't need to complicate my life more than it already was. Chowen laughed.

"Okay, but we'll probably end up in VIP." I felt the pill I had taken in the limo-bus kick in. If I wasn't already sitting, I would have fallen over. The club became blurry and my neck had difficulty supporting my head. I breathed in slowly and held on to the armrests until the wave subsided.

A few more dancers came by, but I was more interested in being high.

Chowen leaned over to me. "Find a girl you like and get a dance." I didn't want to find a girl and I didn't want a dance, but I was also the only one at our table not socializing for fear it would interrupt my high.

Chowen waved over one of the bouncers who called himself "L." L was a large, black man with a friendly smile and a fitted suit. He put his arm around me and leaned in close to hear me speak.

"Whaddya like?" he asked.

"Umm, petit," was all I could come up with. Perrine

was petit. I missed her even then. I thought about how she would have found this entire escapade ridiculously funny if I weren't hurting her so much.

"Okay, Mister Rob, I think I can help you," L assured me before walking away. L returned a few minutes later with a gorgeous, petite woman wearing red lace lingerie. She had long brown hair and dark piercing eyes that looked right into mine. She smiled and sat in my lap while she wrapped her arms around me.

"What's your name?" she asked.

"Rob. You?"

"I'm Theresa. Nice to meet you, Rob. Where you from?"

"Canada"

"Oh, wow. I love Canadians. Everyone I meet from there is always so nice. What city?"

"Ottawa," I said, not expecting her to know where it was.

"Nice." She didn't know where it was.

"Is Theresa your real name or is it one you use here?" I asked, quickly nervous. "I mean, you don't have to tell me your real name, I was just wondering. Rob is my real name in case you're wondering."

I tried to be funny, still struggling to hide how high I was. At first, I felt Theresa lean back, but she quelled my fears with a laugh.

"No, it's not my real name. It's just for privacy. My name's Nicole, but my friends call me Nikki." I wasn't sure if this was another tool in the dancer toolkit. Revealing their real name, or another alias could be a way to connect a little more, which would garner loyalty and thus more willingness to pay for dances or VIP rooms.

"What's it like to work here?" I wondered how seemingly normal people like Nikki could end up taking her clothes off for money. Was it something some people choose to do because they enjoyed it, or was it a means to an end? Was I being presumptuous in assuming that all erotic dancers were lost souls? Contemplating the life predicament of erotic dancers helped shift the focus off my own. Maybe finding another lost soul to spend time with wasn't the worst idea.

"It's not bad. I work two or three nights a week and the money's really good. Most people are pretty nice. Sometimes there's creeps, but security is pretty tight. You seem nice, plus you're good looking which is always much better." Nikki laughed.

I smiled and felt my face warm. I couldn't tell if she was serious, but I soon realized that Nikki was a professional who recognized that I was high and knew to massage my hands and shoulders. We got quiet and my eyes closed. Her hands moved slowly and deeply into the base of my neck. The music slowed and I felt a dozen hands gliding, rubbing every inch of my body. My eyes opened abruptly. The music went back to normal. I saw Chowen look over to us while another dancer danced for him.

"You're rolling hard," Nikki whispered in my ear.

"Rolling" means high on Ecstasy. Add another credit to my Vegas University degree.

"I am," I smiled as she continued to rub my neck.

"Want to grab a VIP room?" Nikki asked. Taking a quick self-inventory, I knew that I was in a new city, pretty drunk, very high, and probably shouldn't separate from the guys. I also had no idea where I was or how I would get back to the hotel making the proposition a terrible idea.

"Yes," I responded. Chowen chuckled. He knew what was going on. He was going to the same place. As we stood up, he handed me another half pill. I looked at it and thought of Perrine. I didn't want to think about Perrine. I didn't want to think about my life and what I had to go back to. I swallowed the pill quickly and couldn't wait for it to kick in.

Nikki led me into the VIP area where there was another set of bouncers and cashiers. Another muscle-bound bouncer, who must have been six and a half feet tall, sat in front of a register at the entryway of the VIP. "Want to go for an hour?" he asked, looking at me unimpressed. I stood there without saying a word. "It's four hundred dollars an hour, plus you have to buy two drinks." Nikki looked at me and smiled. It was a "what did you expect?" kind of smile. I had no idea what to expect.

"Sounds good," I shrugged, and we embarked on the most convoluted payment process I'd ever experienced. The process began with me pulling out my credit card, a challenge in itself in my given state, and I didn't want to lose that feeling before I got to the VIP room. The credit card was taken, and I was handed a receipt on which I could add a tip for the bouncer and his trusted cashier. Not tipping was considered rude, and why wouldn't I tip someone I had just met and uttered four words to? After I filled in the amount, the bouncer pulled out an ink-pad and asked for my thumb. "You're taking my fingerprints?" I recall saying as my thumb was pressed onto the receipt. The bouncer didn't dignify me with an answer. He didn't even look up. Finally, Nikki took my hand and led me to our area.

The VIP room wasn't what I had envisioned. Of course, I hadn't really thought I'd end up in one. It wasn't a private room, rather a set of semi-private booths where patrons could sit back while the dancers used the open space to maneuver. Rick and Chowen chatted with their dancers across from me. I ordered another rum and Diet Coke and a glass of champagne for Nikki who sat beside me. We continued our conversation about her work and my life back home when she began to remove my belt. I immediately looked around to see if anyone else was having sex in the room, but no one was. Nikki said that removing my belt was as much for her as it was for me. Belts get in the way of close rubbing and can affect dancers' skin in sensitive places. Off with the belt! An hour went by. The new pill finally kicked in and was followed by a few more hours of dancing, rubbing, talking, and more drinks. When she danced, Nikki looked into my eyes and moved so close her lips brushed against mine.

"Are we allowed to kiss?" I asked. I imagined how a kiss from her would feel at that moment. Nikki smiled and shook her head, but then looked around to see if anyone was watching and kissed me. Our lips touching was the center of my universe.

It felt as if I was flying through a balmy tunnel of pre-orgasmic tingling where gravity didn't exist. I dissolved into the glamorously clichéd world of falling for a stripper. Half-jokingly, I asked her to marry me. Nikki laughed, poking me in the shoulder. "Let's see how you feel tomorrow. If you do want to hang out tomorrow night, I'm down." She put her number into my phone and I promised to text her the next day.

When I looked up, Rick had vanished and Chowen signaled that it was time to go. The drugs were also wearing off. I said goodbye to Nikki and we found our way to the door of the Rhino where a limo was waiting to take us to the hotel. When you spend a lot of money at the Rhino, they make sure you get home safely. I was ill prepared for what I saw when we stepped outside. The sun. It was 9:00 a.m. I was a vampire scurrying to avoid daylight, believing it was going to kill me. I looked to Chowen whose skin was clear and white. I knew I looked the same. The lobby of our hotel, the MGM Grand, was bustling and I felt humiliated at the thought that we were only getting back to our hotel while everyone else was starting their day. I was, however, glad I had gotten a suite with two private bedrooms so that I could pass out alone, in peace. When we walked into the suite, my suite-mate, Joey, had just woken up. "You guys are just getting back now?" He looked surprised, possibly disgusted.

"Yup," I said proudly for some reason. Chowen giggled.

"Want some Gatorade?" asked Joey as he held one up.

"Add some vodka to it," said Chowen. I took the Gatorade without the vodka. We had our drink then decided to rest up. We still had another entire night left in Vegas.

I woke to voices and grown men shaking my bed. It was 5:00 p.m. and my head was pounding. There was no way I was leaving the hotel room. Rattling pulsed from the night table. My phone sat impatiently waiting to tell me about the dozens of texts and missed phone calls from Perrine. She was worried and pissed. Assumedly more of the latter. When I responded to her texts and called her, she was surprisingly understanding. Her trust in me punched me in the solar plexus. Perrine still didn't truly accept that we were headed towards separation. I remained too much of a coward to quell the hope she still held. Maybe I, too, held hope somewhere deep down and contrary to my new strip club patron self. I told her I was having fun and explained that I got drunk and passed out to which she LOL'd. We said goodbye and I said I would call her the next day.

After I hung up, I saw I had missed some texts from Nikki. She said she was going to work and to come by after the club again. I had a feeling that this was another play in the dancer's playbook. Flirt your way into the patron's phone so you can text them and lure them back in to spend more money. I didn't care. It's not like I'd asked her to marry me.

The plan for the night was the same as the night before. We would hit another club and get bottle service and a limo to the Rhino afterward. All I could think about was how awful a person I was for doing so many drugs and kissing Nikki, while Perrine called me to make sure I was okay despite our disintegrating marriage. The comedown from the ecstasy amplified my depression. I was anxious to ascend to the altitude of last night's high. My body felt like it was trying to reject the oxygen in the air while I broadcasted smiles and raised my glass in a toast to the man of honor. As soon as the dinner was over, Chowen and I each swallowed our first pill—a whole pill. No more halves for us. I needed to find my way back to the nirvana I found the night before. To the world that didn't know me. It wasn't about the drugs, or Nikki, or Chowen. It wasn't about being there for my new friends. It was about not being the person in so much pain. It was about the fact that I was embracing becoming a pathetic selfish victim.

Other than attending a UFC fight, the night was a reasonable facsimile of the night before. Stumbling around in a nightclub surrounded by strangers, swallowing pill after pill, followed by another stop at the Rhino where

Nikki was waiting. We repeated the previous night's expensive consultation in the VIP room. Alone once more, Chowen and I made our way home in the morning sunlight and considered climbing into bed to sleep, but it was too late. There was a day club party waiting and our attendance was mandatory.

A day club is similar to a nightclub in that it serves alcohol and has booths with bottle service. Day clubs just happen during the day in the sunlight around a pool. Our day club of choice, Wet Republic, was conveniently situated on the hotel's property where we were staying. Months earlier when booking my flights, I hadn't considered wanting to spend more time in Las Vegas than absolutely necessary. I decided to join the group at the day club for a drink before heading to the airport. What's the worst that can happen? For fear of my oncoming comedown, and some advice from new and existing alcohol in my bloodstream, I swallowed more pills. I called the airline to change my flight. I had no plan on how to explain my change to Perrine.

I didn't stop to think about where I would sleep. My bags were already checked out of my room and being held at the front desk. I decided I would figure it out later and stayed with the group who laughed at who I had become. They gave me high fives in celebration of my new incautious, party boy persona. My reciprocation served to further repress the guilt building within. This is who I am now. It wasn't right for me and definitely wasn't right for Perrine. I needed to escape deeper into oblivion, deeper into depression, closer to letting go.

After the day club, I staggered through the blurry stain covered casino carpeting to Chowen's hotel room where I stowed my luggage. After a half-successful attempt at inducing a few hours of sleep-like stillness, we crawled up from the buzzing unrest. We didn't bother eating. Ecstasy has a way of killing any hunger cravings and even if I had a craving for food, its smell once placed in front of me was repulsive. We cleaned ourselves up and headed to the hotel bar.

After a few rounds of drinks and pills, a couple of ladies joined us. I struck up a great conversation with one, Andrea, who told me about her father who was a senator in Hawaii. Andrea had shoulder-length dark hair and leaned in close when she spoke. She and her friend asked if I wanted to go home with them which confused me. Chowen looked at me sternly, shook his head, and mouthed the word "no" very slowly. I agreed to go home with them not knowing where the night would take me but Chowen interceded.

"They're working," he whispered in my ear.

"Working?"

"Prostitutes," said Chowen, shaking his head. I didn't believe him, and the girls interrupted our private discussion. With no tact or filter in my high, drunk state I blurted out, "He said you're working." Andrea turned to Chowen and slapped him across the face. Hard. Chowen took the shot and took a breath. Seemingly annoyed at my betrayal, he forced a smile, put up his hands, and walked away as if to say, "It's your call, Rob."

A moment later I found myself outside of the club alone with these two strange women. The three of us started walking through the casino, each of them with a hold of one of my arms. I saw them smirk to each other out of the corner of my eye. I stopped walking, apologized to the girls, and went back to my friends. Chowen shook his head as I walked back into the club. He forgave me, playfully teasing me about it the rest of the night.

After the club, we paid another visit to the Spearmint Rhino. Nikki wasn't there, but I still yearned for the manufactured connection I felt the first night with her. Who it was with didn't matter. I longed to believe that I wasn't alone even if I was. Even if I had to pay for it. The flight that I had rescheduled meant I had to be at the airport at eight the next morning. Chowen stepped up and showed some responsibility. He told L, our bouncer once more, to make sure I didn't miss my flight.

It was a slow Sunday night at the Rhino. Dancers swarmed, gyrated, hurtled, and bounced their bodies over us. A few more drinks, a few more pills, and we were back in VIP with a couple of new girls. Chowen and I perched back on the deep, brown leather bench while our laps hosted our new naked friends. Mine was named "Star."

"Can we kiss?" I asked almost as soon as we sat down.

"That's against the rules," Star said, delivering a flirty, yet dismissive, answer. Her eyes studied the rest of the room unimpressed, an expression she was little concerned to hide, as her thighs straddled my lap and her breasts slid against my face. Not even Ecstasy could conceal her demeanor.

"Some dancers kiss," I tried again.

"I'm sure they do." Her tone ceased our exchange. I remained a simple patron who unenthusiastically accepted delivery of his service. Even though I had Perrine, even though I had friends and family who loved me back home, I reduced myself to a desperate, lonely loser who could only find, who only deserved, a frigid, fake interaction.

"Mister Rob," L said as he leaned into the booth from behind the curtain. I looked at him and tried to focus my eyes. "It's time. I have a limo waiting for you." I hugged Chowen goodbye and walked out into the blinding Las Vegas sun.

* * *

At the airport, I was able to fumble my way through check-in and made my way to security. A new pulse of panic shocked my body into high alert. For most of the weekend, I had ecstasy in my pockets. These pills were hidden in various places over my body to ensure security at the clubs wouldn't find them. Given my state, I couldn't remember where all these hiding places were. I was sure that the scanning machine would pick up one of these areas and I would be found out. That would be it for me. *Entrepreneur arrested for possession of Class A narcotics. The suspect was unable to comment due to how fucked up he was when arrested.* Classy, Rob, classy. I was now a guy licking his painfully chapped lips, darting his eyes around, suspiciously feeling every crevice of his jeans and shirt while barely able to balance himself on his feet in the security line. I was an arrest waiting to happen. Then I was *anomalously selected* to enter the air blowing "puffer" machine. "This is it," I thought to myself. I took a deep breath and walked into the machine. A squawking noise, not unlike the off-camera adults of Charlie Brown cartoons, pierced its way into my eardrums. I turned to see a tall, slightly agitated security woman trying to get my attention.

"Sir...SIR!" I innocently smiled at her. "You have to put your hands up," her voice rose above the chatter of the crowd. Dozens, which felt like thousands, of onlookers scrutinized my behavior. I turned back in shame confusing her direction of how I should be standing in the machine and putting my hands up to be arrested. The officer pointed back to the machine floor once again where I was to stand on two yellow footprints. Relieved, I stepped into the machine. I heard no sound. The machine's tentacles circled me, shooting their judgmental breaths searching for the drugs I was sure I had forgotten. "Okay, step here." The officer motioned to me to retrieve my things and be on my way. They found nothing. There was nothing to be found. I was simply another wayward drunkard being processed through security at the Las Vegas airport at 7:00 a.m. on a Monday.

I ran off to my gate where I sat in silence until I could get on the plane. I passed out on the flight only to be awakened by a flight attendant who, in her best non-judgmental yet completely judgmental way, let me know I had to leave. I was the last passenger on the plane.

The weekend in Las Vegas brought with it a new escape. I now had a way to alleviate the pain. Ecstasy showed me the door and all I had to do was walk through it. I sprinted. Perrine had no idea and I wasn't planning on telling her. I wondered what Kevin would think of all this drug business. He knew I would never leave him, but I wondered if he'd feel different about me. He was waiting for me when I returned home. We said nothing.

The Stink of Apartments

I WAS BORN IN THE SOUTH SHORE OF MONTREAL IN 1972 shortly after my parents married. They were twenty years old then. When I consider my immaturity at twenty, it seems to be irresponsibly young to be parents. I was too immature to have a baby when I was thirty, let alone twenty. I attribute their youth to the fact that my parents rarely, if ever, taught me the many necessities I would need for my journey through life. I was a blank canvas upon which there was no paint. Instead I was left to figure things out by watching the unremarkable adults in my parents' lives and through television characters who didn't exist in the real world: the positive influences like Gordon and Luis from Sesame Street to the unachievable, supportive family dynamics of the Brady Bunch, to the ridiculous shenanigans of Gilligan's Island. Most of the village that raised me lived in the television set.

Like most dysfunctional families, each of my parents' upbringings had their respective sets of issues—estrangements between siblings and parents, alcoholism, drug addiction—along with a litany of verbal and physical abuse sprinkled in for good measure. Each of my parents married three times. Each of them divorced as often.

When I was a toddler, Mom secretly borrowed money from a friend and took me without telling my father. We moved to Hamilton, a six-hour drive away from Montreal. Dad was not pleased. Against the advice of her lawyer, Mom refused to ask my father for monetary support for fear of a legal battle that could jeopardize her non-state-endorsed sole custody of me. When it came to visitation, they agreed that I'd stay with Dad twice a year: a six-week visit during my summer break from school and one week at Christmas.

My trips to Montreal became an escape from the friendless and borderline destitute conditions in which I was living. I bragged to anyone who would listen about how I was going to visit my rich father in the exciting big city of Montreal. He was not rich, but they didn't know. Dad lived in a quiet neighborhood in a middle-class house with two bathrooms, which to me was luxury. The flights back and forth were fun adventures in and of themselves for a five-year-old. My mom handed me off in tears to a beautiful flight attendant who escorted me aboard the aircraft—which, back then, wasn't a far walk as anyone could walk up to any gate in the airport. The flight attendant took me to my seat where I'd invariably order a ginger ale. Unfortunately, it was a time when smoking was still allowed on airliners. From an early age, I despised smoking, feeling an instinctive embarrassment and disgust whenever my mother or father lit up. I still have visions of my Mom's lit cigarette dangling from her mouth as she knelt in front of me, zipping up my winter jacket while my face tried desperately to lean away from the clouds of smoke.

My father remarried and I was excited to visit his new wife, Carol. Carol was kind and gentle with a loud, articulate voice that echoed through the house when she laughed. I'm not sure if she knew I was a part of the deal when she and my Dad married, but during those summers when he was at work all day, it was Carol who looked after me. We baked Toll House cookies together, and she taught me how to play Johann Pachelbel's Canon in D Major on the piano. I couldn't read the music but was able to play by memorizing the sequence and timing of the keys. I practiced enough for it to sound like I knew what I was doing, but if I tried to play any other song it would sound like a limping cat was walking across the keys.

There was sadness in Carol's eyes when she didn't know I was watching. Inevitably she felt my stare and abruptly forced out a smile. The fake smile confused me for a long time, but I never asked for fear that asking might result in her not being as kind to me anymore.

Life was different back in Hamilton, but although

we didn't have much in the way of material things, Mom was very affectionate and loving. She kept me physically close almost all the time, and tucked me in with the same words that I would repeat back to her every night. "Good night," she would start.

"Good night," I'd respond with a smile.

"See you in the morning."

"See you in the morning."

"I love you."

"I love you," I finished as she kissed my forehead. I looked forward to the nightly routine that helped put me to sleep in those early years.

The lack of child support was a significant setback and left us near-destitute moving from one shitty apartment to another shitty apartment, sometimes relying on family or local charities for food. The buildings we lived in varied in their location, but were all the same. All had filthy hallways with pungent smells of bad foreign cooking and body odor. All had broken doors in the entrances so anyone could walk in and all these apartments had small bedrooms and one bathroom. My mother was a tidy person, but her cleanliness only kept the bugs at bay. Once the lights were out, the creepy-crawlies held festivals and scurried away if a light was turned on. Most of them anyway.

Mom wasn't held back for too long though. She took over a hair salon from her cousin and it began to thrive. This helped our financial condition, but at a cost. Mom was working fifty-plus hours a week. I was now under the care of a new village consisting of my mother's revolving circle of friends and, if I was lucky, family. It also meant increased time alone at home when I was far too young. Fortunately, this was a time of LEGO and *Star Wars*. Whenever I was alone, I poured out my collection of colorful LEGO blocks and began to build, or if *Star Wars* was on one of the pay-per-view channels, I watched it fixedly through the scrambled flicker of the screen. We couldn't afford to pay for those channels, but I didn't mind. I knew every scene, every line. For those few hours, I was the lost child Luke Skywalker, the irresponsible thief Han Solo, the lonely hermit Yoda. The diversion of *Star Wars* and LEGO were safe places to hide. Places I projected myself into to forget a reality that I could not yet process.

A couple of years after Mom left my father, she met a new man, Joe. Joe was a fun, young musician who played with me as if he was a cool older brother. He was tall and liked basketball, and he bought me one. We'd go outside to the parking lot where he taught me how to dribble and, even without a hoop, played for hours. He told me jokes and wrestled with me on the sofas. I also appreciated the fact that he didn't smoke.

I was five when Joe and Mom were married and I was left to my own devices at the wedding reception. I don't know who but someone thought it would be cute to let me have a taste of champagne during one of the toasts. I loved it immediately and tried to find more. Any attempts from adults to thwart my drinking only led to sharpen my resolve. I was small and nimble and they were old and drunk. I inhaled the contents of all the near-empty cups on the tables before anyone could stop me. After a particularly bitter tasting shot of champagne, I discovered cigarette butts at the bottom. I was found vomiting in a urinal in the men's room, much to the disgust of lookers-on who scowled and didn't help.

When I managed to get back into the reception, someone asked who I would be staying with while Mom and Joe would be away on their honeymoon. *Honeymoon? What's a honeymoon?* My inebriated five-year-old brain could not comprehend the question. Mom was going somewhere without me? I was "staying with someone???" Panicked, I ran to her to ask what was going on but it was too late. They were already leaving and I was to be cared for by my mother's cousin—a cousin I did not know very well. I was to stay at a place I had never been. I was a drunk, sick, five-year-old abandoned with a stranger. Mom blew me a kiss as she left and I reached out to her crying. In a tear-soaked blink, she was gone. I was not good company for my mother's cousin and was left in a room for many hours—thankfully with LEGO blocks.

Joe and Mom led a life filled with parties and Mom's salon, left neglected, began to fail. Once again, we struggled to make ends meet financially. Joe worked at a steel factory and played music on weekends while Mom cut hair in our kitchen. They still found time to socialize at night, however. Mom and Joe brought me along to parties where they drank, smoked, and played cards with their friends. Each time, I'd fall asleep on someone's couch only to be jolted awake every few minutes by waves of screaming laughter, making it impossible to fall into a deep rest. It was as if they were trying to torture me by letting me fall asleep with only the sound of playing cards hitting the table, only to pour freezing water over me and laughing to add insult to injury. Worse, the smell of every cigarette they lit wafted into my sinuses, leaving me to smother in the smoke in those dank, small, shitty apartments.

At the end of the night, Joe carried me to his rusted white Mercury Cougar where I'd lie across the back seat. There were no car seats back then, and I have no idea how sober they were, but the ride home was my favorite part of these nights. The air always crisp and breezy and, combined with the sound and vibration of the car and my exhaustion, I went to a dream-like, half-conscious world. Traffic lights flashed by in the night sky and I covered my eyes with anything I could find, like the sleeve of a jacket or a wayward seat belt. When we arrived home and Joe laid me in bed, the silence shook me awake, but it wouldn't take long for me to drift into a slumber.

There was a brief discussion about Joe adopting me, but my father wouldn't have it. He told me that he loved me too much to let me go. It overwhelmed me to hear that even at such a young age. Rejecting the adoption turned out to be a good thing because Mom and Joe didn't last. Mom and I were on our own again. She began to party more often and more than once we hosted a new "uncle" at breakfast, or one who may have simply said hello on his way out in the morning. One of these "uncles" was the man who raped me.

Merry Vegas

"I THINK IT'D BE BEST IF WE SPLIT UP." BEADS OF TEAR-drops rolled down my face as I said the words. We were back on the oversized sofa in our living room. Perrine and I looked at each other, both of us exhausted. It was only a few weeks after my trip to Las Vegas.

"Okay, I'm not going to push anymore." Perrine had finally given up. "I thought if we could tough it out until you could get some help, we could make it, but you've given up. It sucks." She hugged me tightly.

"It sucks," I whispered. We cried until Perrine stood up and walked out of the room. I looked at Spring who crawled over and sat on my lap. I petted him and heard Kevin's voice.

"It had to happen, man, sorry."

"Fuck you."

The symphony of alcohol, drugs, music, and self-destruction in Las Vegas pulled me into an entirely new world—the Electronic Dance Music, or EDM, scene. In the Eighties I pledged no allegiance to a genre, nor did any of it define me. With the music of my Vegas nightclub experience interwoven with the high of Ecstasy, I made an effort to learn more about the artists. I was captivated by Avicii's "Levels" track when I heard it at Rain Nightclub in the Palms. It made me cheerful amidst the pain of my reality. I found Avicci's Levels podcast which led me to Tiesto, Swedish House Mafia, Kaskade, Sander van Doorn and many more. I listened in my car, at work, and while I worked at home. House music became the theme music to mundane tasks like showering, eating, and getting ready in the morning. I'd danced around my condo reminiscing of my last high. The distraction prevented any unnecessary rumination of the pain still prevalent in the real world. It prevented any chance to face it or heal.

Near the end of our first Vegas meeting, Chowen and I decided that we needed a trip for just the two of us. He wanted the same escape and loved the same drugs I did. If I was with Chowen, I didn't have to drown alone and we didn't have to pretend everything was okay. Chowen lived in Winnipeg, over two thousand kilometers away from Ottawa, making it difficult to see each other very often—probably a good thing given our mutual tendency and enablement for self-destruction. We agreed to meet in Vegas as Avicii was DJing live at one of the world's best clubs, Club XS in the Wynn Hotel.

I nearly fell to the ground when the first wave of Ecstasy kicked in as we walked into Club XS. Every light, every sparkle, every reflection was a spotlight pulsing into my retinas. Each drop in the music punched me in the chest. The club was crowded and intimidating, but I was too high to care. Chowen and I danced around and talked to people for hours, but we were only biding our time until we went back to the Rhino. I was looking forward to reconnecting with Nikki and reliving our last experience. I did see Nikki, but it wasn't the same. I could barely speak from all the Ecstasy, but that didn't stop us from finding ourselves back in the VIP. I remembered nothing and was left with only the line items on my credit card statement and ink on my thumb.

Two more nights followed the same pattern, yet somehow I managed to make it back on the correct flight home. Unlike my first Vegas adventure, I had not let myself become sober the entire weekend. Instead of many smaller comedowns, I began feeling the effects of one big one. As I sat down in my assigned middle seat for my flight home, I was now severely chemically imbalanced. I began having trouble inhaling. I forced a deep breath. Trying to appear calm, I looked around to see if any passengers were watching.

On the outside, I looked like a meditative sloth; on the inside, I was a Tasmanian Devil on meth. My mind came up with scenarios of police coming on board and dragging me to jail. How would this look to my family and friends? I started to hate myself for doing drugs at all. I staved back the tears. Gripping the armrests tightly,

I waited for the seat belt sign to turn off. I made my way to the washroom and locked the door. I looked at myself in the mirror for the first time in days and examined my bloodshot eyes, my pale white skin, my face thinning from dehydration. I sobbed. I fell back on the toilet and cried uncontrollably. The background hum of the plane held a grip on my entire body squeezing me with every slight tremor. It wasn't the plane; it was the convulsions from the come down. In the seconds it subsided, my mind flashed to my reality. I pushed away the love of my life back home. All I wanted to do was forget but the vibration tormented me. Pounding knocks on the door thrust me back into the present. I took a few more deep breaths. I cleaned myself up, regained composure, and walked back to my seat. The crying allowed me to go into a daze for the duration of the flight.

I landed in Salt Lake City for a layover and the fun continued. Distraught and in a rough haze, I could no longer read the signs in the terminal making it impossible to find my next gate. Too paranoid to ask anyone for help, I decided to sit on a nearby bench. As soon as I considered the thought of sitting, my body began to shut down. I made it to a wall and slid to the ground. A security guard walked by and I motioned I was plugging in my phone charger to an outlet near me. He continued to walk by.

My paranoia descended from a fifteen to fourteen out of ten. I examined my boarding pass closely for what felt like an hour and identified where I needed to go. I tried to calm down and relax. I passed out. I woke up to a damp, drool-soaked shoulder. When I figured out where I was, I checked my boarding pass and then the time. Fuck! I missed my flight. Adrenaline kicked in again and I jumped to my feet. I found my way to a counter to purchase the next flight home—six hours later. Fuck again. At some point, I got on a plane and made it to my house safely. Kevin was there waiting. He was confused which made me confused. All these years Kevin always knew what to do. I knew that I had sunk to a new low, but I didn't want to talk about it. I waved a we'll-talk-later wave and fell into bed. It took weeks to feel normal again, but I was far from normal.

My sister, Michelle, was a beautiful young woman with voluminous dark hair and kind, hazel eyes. At their own risk, my friends reminded me of her beauty. We only saw each other a few times a year but we kept a strong connection. Moreover, although we looked forward to spending time together, we felt the same abhorrence for our anxiety-riddled family functions such as Christmas. It was only a few months after my breakup with Perrine when the thought of being at another forced, uncomfortable family Christmas shot pains in my stomach. I wanted to do the exact opposite of what our family expected and came up with a ridiculous, albeit uncreative, idea: Vegas. Not yet aware of the depths to which I had sunk and not wanting me to be alone, Michelle agreed to join me. I let the rest of the family know without a second thought. Christmas would never be the same.

Christmas Eve we ended up at the TAO Nightclub. Michelle wasn't new to Ecstasy. She knew enough to nibble a half or a quarter pill, get a little high, and maintain composure. That was a skill so foreign to me I didn't even question it. I popped a couple of pills, Michelle a half pill, and we chased them down with drinks—my usual rum and Diet Coke, and she with a glass of champagne. When the drugs kicked in, we found our way to the dance floor and let the music take us, smiling at each other as if sharing a private joke. I went to get us more drinks and when I returned I found a man talking with Michelle. He invited us to the bottle service booth he shared with friends, a group of forty-somethings from Orange County, California. I met a large-set man wearing a draping white, wrinkled, short-sleeved dress shirt that hung over his jeans. His shirt was unbuttoned at the top, revealing thick gold chains that matched his oversized gold watch and rings. He was sweating profusely. I assumed he was high on Ecstasy like me.

"This bottle of Hennessy is almost *ten times* the price here!" His objection seemed to be more bragging than complaining. "At least we have gorgeous women fetch it for us," he said, pointing to his server. We continued our conversation with the requisite disclosure of our respective professions, cities of residence, and what cars we drove. The friends generously poured us more drinks while we danced and laughed together. When the night was almost over, they invited us over to do some shots to finish the remaining alcohol. I was a few pills and many drinks in already, but to decline would be rude. We downed the shots. A lot of shots. They were laughing. We were laughing. We said goodbye and embarked on our long walk back to the hotel.

As we left the club, I started to get dizzy. Up until that point, I was getting used to the feeling of being high, drunk, and the inevitable comedown, but this was different. My body started tingling, and it felt as if I was floating while trying to keep my feet on the ground. I turned to Michelle. I could barely make out her silhouette. I had trouble speaking and felt cold sweat seeping from my warm skin. I heard Michelle's voice from a distance.

"My feet are going to throw up," she said. I processed her statement with my confused mind, wondering if she was as high as I was or if it was one of her witty jokes. It turned out that it was both. "I don't feel right," she added.

"Yeah, I'm pretty messed up." I looked down to confirm my feet remained on solid ground. That's when it dawned on us both—there had been drugs in those liquor bottles. GHB to be exact. In small doses GHB, or Gamma-Hydroxybutyrate, can cause euphoria and dizziness. But it's also known as the "date rape" drug because an effective dose can cause loss of consciousness and erase your memory. The guy Michelle was talking to mentioned they were high on it, but we didn't know it was in the bottles. It now made sense why the man I was talking to was drenched in sweat. It was a drug I had never done before and knew very little about. I didn't like it. I wasn't in control. I desperately needed to get back to our hotel room. After a few missteps and only one (or possibly more) wipeouts, we made it to the elevators. We crawled from the elevator to our room where we passed out. My stomach felt ready to erupt, but I couldn't vomit. I longed for the comfort of my melting ceilings.

When we woke up the next afternoon, my body was confused. It wondered why it was still alive despite my best attempts at drowning the remaining life left in it. Michelle and I didn't talk about why we were in Vegas, or why I had recently started taking drugs. She knew I was upset about my break up with Perrine, but didn't know why and she didn't ask.

The Scene

MY HOMETOWN OF OTTAWA IS A MEDIUM-SIZE CITY WITH
a population comparable to Boston. There aren't as many
nightclubs as there are sit-down-and-get-drunk bars,
also like Boston. I've found one would be hard-pressed
to find any real discourse in nightclubs in any city. Intel-
lectuals tend not to assemble in places where the music
overwhelms any attempted discussion of thoughts and
ideas. Conversations, if one could call them that, are indi-
viduals waiting for their turn to speak in order to best
the previous speaker, or worse, an attempt to broadcast
a mating signal.

"Dude, I made a million dollars last year!" a friend
shouted. His eyes looked passed me. The proclamation
was without context. Confused, I was about to ask why
he said it so loudly, when he grabbed my shoulders
and repositioned me a few steps back. When I turned
around, I saw that we had moved within earshot of two
women standing behind me. "Dude, I made a million

dollars last year!" Satisfied the ladies had heard his pronouncement, he raised his glass expectantly. I tapped my glass against his. I wondered what kind of woman he was after. What kind of person would be so shallow as to pursue someone based on money alone? Why was my friend stooping to this level? He was good-looking with an abundance of charisma and wit. Did he need to be rich too? It was clear that the game he was playing wasn't about finding a lifelong partner. For some men, it was a catch and release sport. If the man "scores," his ego is appeased for the night. For the woman, she had access to the material things that attracted her for a short while. Things got messy when one of these players was looking for something real when the other one wasn't.

I had trouble navigating these waters. I wasn't confident, or egregious enough to boast about what I had nor did I want to. I just wanted to be high or drunk, or ideally both, and not physically alone. Admittedly, I was envious of my charismatic friend and his ability to attract beautiful women, even if he was full of shit. I could play this game, I thought. I had things I could show off. It's not like I was too good to be a dirtbag. I'd lied to, cheated on, and hurt every person in my life so far. Shit, I'd earned the dirtbag merit badge. I hated who I was becoming, but I still chose to go further down the rabbit hole. The worse I became, the more I'd hate myself, and the easier it would be to end my life.

* * *

I had to get out of the house. I was still living in the matrimonial home Perrine and I had purchased together. Being alone in the house we believed we would raise children in served as a constant reminder of that terrible night of revelation, and the subsequent loss of the woman I loved. On weekends, I started to go out for dinner and drinks with whomever would say yes. These nights invariably parlayed into more drinks and then on to one of the local nightclubs. There were different clubs for different friends. Some liked the cheap dollar-a-beer bars that ended with many drunk and "willing" women. Conversations on those nights focused on how best to attract and pick up girls. If I engaged in any sort of conversation outside of angling women, the topic would quickly dissolve into the smoky air of the bar.

Other friends preferred the high-class clubs where the patronage dressed up and talked about themselves, their work, and how much money they had. Although I preferred the high-class Vegas-esque scene, I despised talking about money because it made people think I had far more than I did. To be fair, I had a Lamborghini then and parked it in front of the club. A dick ego move, yes, but it fast-forwarded my "street-cred" gaining me access to front of the lines and invites to the next party. I was always friendly but relatively quiet, which helped me as well.

Somehow, I met Branson, the owner of the best night-clubs in Ottawa. Branson was a good-looking Lebanese man, not much older than me. He greeted people in the bar with an infectious smile, warm hugs, and two-handed handshakes. Branson began his career co-founding a popular men's magazine, which he continued to run along with the clubs he owned. He'd regularly bring in celebrities to hang out in his clubs. Many women who met Branson bragged how they "knew the owner." Some would flirt their way into his inner circle and tried to be his girl, to no avail.

I became a regular at his clubs, and Branson and I developed a friendship. On Thursdays and Saturdays we'd go to a trendy place for dinner, then drinks at local hot spots. Without fail he would find and invite a tableful of ladies to join us at the club that night. Many times, they would. On Sundays, we met for recovery breakfasts or brunches while we talked about life.

"Do you ever get sick of it?" I looked at Branson sitting across from me. We were sitting quietly on a restaurant patio, nursing our hangovers with coffee and staring blankly at plates of uneaten food. "Partying, I mean." Branson sighed and looked me in the eye.

"Every weekend." The answer surprised me. Branson always looked so energized and content in the spotlight of the club. "It's like an addiction. The hot twenty-somethings all over you all the time. I'm treated like a celebrity." He paused. "But I know it's fake. I'll get out soon. Probably within a year. I'll sell the club to the staff and disappear from the scene. I'm making plans." I felt he was trying to convince himself as much as he was trying to convince me. "What about you?"

"Me?" I gave him the deflection. "I just don't like being alone at home." The statement surprised me as much as it did him. I looked back at my food and started eating, hoping Branson wouldn't pursue the conversation.

"I know what you mean." Branson revealed a sliver of vulnerability and compassion under his glamourous façade. He knew why people crowded his clubs and it wasn't all about having a good time, especially for the regulars. Some went looking for someone to connect with; some unhappy with their lives needed the escape. Most were lost like me. I found a tribe with which the only thing we had in common was that we were lost. In the moment, we were sloppily high-fiving, professing our love for each other. But when the moments were over, when we were alone with ourselves, our phones and social media became the methadone that fought off any sober self-examination.

Branson introduced me to many of his friends, which included high profile businesspeople, local celebrities and, of course, lots of women. It became a comedy routine. Branson would grab me and pull me over to one or two women and say, "This is Rob. He is the NICEST, NICEST, NICEST guy!!" And laugh. He told me that being intro-duced as "nice" was not sexy. Women in the club weren't looking for nice. I laughed while he would add, "But don't worry, Rob isn't nice all the time." It proved to be an effective icebreaker and invariably led to the question, "Well, are you nice or not?" Delivered with a flirtatious grin. My response would always be something cheesy like, "I guess we'll have to see." I wasn't interviewing for a job at NASA here nor was I looking for any real connection. I was playing the game Branson was teaching me. Most of the time any conversations I had with women I met in the club led to an eye-roll or them simply walking away. I wasn't very good at the game, at least not without drugs which I promised myself I would not do in my hometown for fear of being found out.

Being friends with Branson came with benefits I didn't expect. I never waited in line at his clubs. I would rarely if ever pay for a drink, and when I tried was denied. Branson felt it was an insult as I was his guest. One may think the impression I was giving with the fancy car and clothes was that I was a big spender, and Branson was looking to leverage that. *If a successful guy like Rob parties here, you should, too.* I wasn't quite that special, however. Far from it. I believe he paid for me because I was his friend. We spent many nights together drinking in his club. Since neither Branson nor I wanted to be with anyone at all, we wouldn't take women home after the club. Instead, we found somewhere to eat. We must've shared a hundred post-club meals together.

Then along came Molly. Molly, aka M or the Love

Drug, was the new name people were using for Ecstasy. The belief was that Molly was "pure" MDMA, while Ecstasy was MDMA mixed with speed or any other cheap/fun additives—even heroin. I was in love with the 'Love Drug.' At first, Vegas was the only place I would take it. But I wanted to do it more, so I looked to meet people who supplied it. I was still too afraid to be high in my own hometown, so I went two hours away to Montreal whenever I could.

As I lost more time spent in clubs, I also lost my regard for discretion. While in my hometown, I began slipping a pill here and there—even when out with Branson, though unbeknownst to him. I convinced myself no one would notice if I was high. My discretion waned in another area, too. Even though I wasn't looking for any real connection, being high on MDMA dissolved my inhibitions and I wanted to experiment sexually. I decided to be radically honest with any woman I met. Radically, brutally, rudely honest.

The first conversation I had with a woman, I'd tell her I was newly divorced, not looking for anything serious, and that I wanted no strings attached fun—oh, and threesomes. At first, it became a way to keep my distance but, unexpectedly, my honesty was more refreshing than rude. It also turned out that many of them had the same curiosities, but were too shy to broach the subject. *Eureka!* Women told me my entire life to be honest and the second I was, I was rewarded.

I believed a threesome was an experience I should want, but I didn't fully know why. Physical sexuality intimidated me to the point of unease before, during, and following the act. Performance anxiety doubled. Yet Molly quickly quelled any emotional side effects. I know I felt love, or perhaps the correct chemical representations of love, during the act but love wasn't a sensation I could consider lasting. Having sex with more than one person was less intimate, and its participants less vulnerable.

As the first opportunity unfolded, I thought taking Molly would simultaneously take the edge off as well as enhance the experience. MDMA removed the negative associations with sex I'd lived with my entire life. The awkwardness, the embarrassment, the shame. MDMA amplified the positive part of sex. The connection, the sensuality, the passion. More than the drug itself, which I adored, I became addicted to being lost in the throes of skin, sweat, penetration, and the chemically-manufactured connection. And that is what it was—manufactured. On the ascent of the chemical bliss, we all loved each other. As the hours went by and the sun started to rise, the shame set in. Each night was a new adventure. Each morning was a new low.

Threesomes became a regular activity, but the Molly brought one challenge. If I did too much, which was nearly every time, erections became increasingly challenging even in the company of two or more women with their clothes off. I added Viagra to the party cocktail. Balancing the highest I could be on Molly with taking too many Viagra was like plate spinning while on a unicycle. Only if a plate fell, I would die of a heart attack.

An irony emerged out of these affairs. While high, we felt like everything in the world was right. Wonderful even. But it wasn't. It wasn't because we were using drugs to deliver us from what was real. Real life wasn't good enough. It was terrible sometimes; for some of us, most times. But rolling together, we were away from that. Afterwards, we remained connected, bonded by an intimate, intense, and depressing experience. We were not limited to the sexual escapades of any drunken club night. Amid our slurred "I love you, man" proclamations, among the whisperings of "Fuck, I am so high," we were together in the trenches. We were on the front lines in the war against loneliness without knowing how to fight it. Together we fought and celebrated by denying our isolation, our sadness, our pain.

Perrine heard that I was out at clubs and getting high. When she asked me about it, I lied and denied most of it. We weren't together, but I lied anyway. I lied because I was embarrassed. I lied because I still placed Perrine on a pedestal. I lied because I knew she still had hope that we would find our way back to each other, and maybe I did too. I hadn't yet accepted that she was becoming increasingly unreachable with every lie I told.

There was never any shortage of reasons to go out and get drunk. Someone's birthday, a long weekend, a nightclub's anniversary, any day ending in "y," or a local event such as Ottawa's annual Food and Wine Festival. The Ottawa Food and Wine Festival was where both club regulars and casual drinkers dressed up to drink as much as their bodies could, and with the predictable results. Ill-fitting, vomit-soaked suits and dresses, wild haymaker punches thrown in drunken brawls, and endless lines of cabs taking the stumbling, drooling masses away. But this particular year provided something far worse.

I met Samantha through a friend. She was a young woman I met at a club that liked to get high as much as I did. Samantha had model-like features. She was tall, thin with long platinum hair and wore a tight, black cocktail dress. She came up to say hello to a friend of mine. She was so inebriated, she could barely stand. Her eyes, which looked around constantly, sat on top of two dark rings only partially covered by her makeup. I asked if she had eaten. Clearly irritated at my question, she managed to slur out, "I ate a piece of sushi at some point." At the end of the Wine and Food Festival, friends invited me to join the limo that would take us to the club to continue the festivities. Nestled in the back seat among several other men, I watched as Samantha crawled her way back to join us. She held a bottle of tequila in her hand and sat in my lap. When she saw the open sunroof, she stood up and danced with the top half of her body in the open air, bottle in hand.

Everyone in the limo dispersed when we reached the

club and I didn't see Samantha again. The night for me continued as usual. I got drunk, high, and went home alone. As the room began to spin me into oblivion, my phone rang. It was the woman I'd gone to the event with. She asked if I had seen Samantha, and I told her I had and when. She thanked me and hung up. Not too long after, she called again. She asked if I could come pick her up. Something had happened and she didn't know what. Despite my lack of sobriety and clear impairment, I said I would and drove the twenty minutes to get her.

When I arrived at her house, she was sobbing uncontrollably. I held her, unable to come up with any comforting words. Between sobbing breaths, she was able to tell me that Samantha had hung herself in her building's private parking lot. I had no idea what to say. I took her to Samantha's house where her friends agreed to meet. When I pulled up to the building, there were police cars parked at the entrance. My friend asked if I could come upstairs with her. I didn't know most of these people. There were police all over the place, and I was still very high and driving. I was also embarrassed. I was almost forty years old and these girls were in their early twenties. When my friend looked at me with her swollen, tear-filled eyes, I felt I had to be there for her. Just as a fellow human in need.

When we entered the apartment, four police officers took notes while five or six girls sat on the sofa talking to them. They all cried while trying to piece together the night. The longer I stayed, the more nervous I grew. Eventually a cop made his way over to me and asked why I was there. I told him I was there to support my friend. He could see I was nervous and took an interest in me, jotting down my name. My name was now a documented part of a suicide investigation. Once the interviews were done, we left. On our way out, we saw Samantha's boyfriend sitting in the front lobby looking dumbfounded. He looked up and acknowledged us with a half wave of his hand. I felt sorry for him but once again words escaped me. I returned a look of condolence and walked away.

Samantha succeeded where I failed. Like me, her friends didn't know how she felt inside. She hid her turmoil in her party life. I wondered how many of us there were. I wondered if she found peace. But mostly I felt jealous that she was able to stop her suffering while I remained too cowardly to do it myself. She was my hero.

Therapy and Other Lies

LESS THAN A YEAR HAD PASSED SINCE THE MEMORY OF the rape had resurfaced. The pain hadn't subsided and neither had the agony of walking away from my marriage. Perrine began dating someone new, but we still kept messaging each other. I continued my spiral downwards, drowning myself in the drunken, high nights of nightclubs, be they in Ottawa, Montreal, or Las Vegas. When I was unable to party or in a state of recovery, I was alone. I filled these gaps of sobriety with the only other thing I knew—work. The new company my friends and I started was taking off and needed my full-time attention. At least, my full-time attention when I was sober. My partners, Mitchel and Jordan, were both younger than me and loved to go out on weekends. They were no strangers to hangovers, which kept my lack of sobriety and crippling drug comedowns well hidden.

Weekdays were long hours at the office followed by more hours of working at home. Many nights I wouldn't bother to turn on the lights when the sun set. The yellow glow of the laptop and the flicker of the TV were the only illumination in my living room. Countless hours sailed by while television shows and movies I wasn't paying attention to bullied the silence out of the room. The steady soundtrack of melodramatic voices and clamorous violence fooled me into believing that I wasn't alone. The nonstop party-work life began wearing on me and I decided to do something I thought I never would, see a therapist. At least it would break the tedium. I didn't believe in therapy because I couldn't understand how talking about events in your past could make them better. The past couldn't be changed. The past should be left alone. Still, I didn't want to be alone and having someone to talk to—possibly be honest with—felt encouraging.

I found Anne online while searching for a suitable therapist. I came by a paper she wrote that intrigued me and saw she had a PhD. Her solid credentials and writing impressed me. For a therapist's magic to work, you have to respect them. *I* have to trust them. Given her acumen, I assumed Anne would work. It took me weeks to summon the courage to schedule an appointment, and after only three or four last minute cancellations, I managed to find my way to her office.

On the way to my first appointment, I entered an old building with a tiny, slow elevator and narrow hallways lit by dim, yellow wall lamps. Anne's office included a small waiting room with three chairs and a coffee table that sat under a stack of dog-eared *National Geographic* magazines. The walls were beige, as was her furniture. I was there early. I sat in one of the beige chairs and picked up one of the old magazines, a refreshing alternative to my smartphone. I heard muffled voices as she ended her session with the patient before me, followed by the sound of a door gently clicking shut. The door to her office opened, and a woman emerged. "Robert?" she asked with a kind smile.

"Yup," I responded, returning the magazine to its brothers on the table and leaning forward to stand.

"I'll be a couple of minutes, but you can come in and sit down," Anne said in a polite, professional voice as she motioned into her office. My stomach tightened and my heart pounded as I stepped in and sat down. Anne walked to a second desk behind me, wrote down some notes and filed them away while I waited. When I scanned the room, I registered movement in the corner. A dog lay curled up in her bed not too far from Anne's desk in front of me. When Anne finished her filing, she sat at her desk. I sat across from her and her dog, a quiet and friendly cocker spaniel. I mentioned how convenient it was that she lived practically across the street from me. Anne's expression turned serious. "I have to tell you that I live in the same building, so if we ever pass each other in the elevator or hallway, I will say hello to you as a neighbour only as to protect your privacy." Taken aback at the delivery I sat quietly trying to process what Anne just told me. It was reassuring to know that my privacy was held at such value.

"OK, makes sense," I acknowledged. "Great commute to work for you, I guess," I joked. Anne gestured a smile. There was minimal small talk. I assumed it was because Anne wanted to make the most of the expensive hour I was paying for.

"I'd like you to write down the goals that you'd like to accomplish with your time here." She handed me a clipboard filled with paper and a pen attached. I wrote down, "I want not to want to die so much," and handed it back to her. Anne read what I had written and looked at me seriously once more. "Do you have this feeling right now?"

I shrugged my shoulders, "Kind of, yes," I said hesitantly. "I'm not planning on hanging myself tonight, but I definitely don't want to live anymore." My knee started to bounce. "And I don't want any drugs to take that feeling away." Ironically, I didn't want to become a drooling zombie or dependent on any drug. I held a deluded notion that not taking a prescribed medication to subdue my death wish would, in some way, allow me to hold on to at least part of my dignity before I was able to achieve it. However, I wanted to keep my beloved Molly for as long as possible and, for that, there was no end in sight.

"If you tell me you are going to hurt yourself, it is my responsibility to contact the police," she stated matter-of-factly. "Is that what you are telling me?" I wasn't sure if she was testing me or giving me an out.

"No, I'm not going to do anything." I took the out. The thought of ending up in a psychiatric hospital so drugged up I couldn't speak—a la Jack Nicholson in *One Flew Over the Cuckoo's Nest*—terrified me.

"Rob, I am here to help you and to do so you will have to be honest with me." It felt as if Anne had pushed me up against the wall where all I could see was her. She seemed to be a person who could see through my bullshit without outright calling it bullshit. "If you ever have those catastrophic thoughts, I want you to write down what led to them in that moment and if you feel you might hurt yourself you can call me directly." She handed me a sheet of paper with contact information and had circled the number in red ink.

I described my current situation to Anne while she took notes without judgment. My heart rate slowed; my stomach settled. With every new fucked up story I told her, she remained professionally aloof. I decided I would go all in and tell her about the rape, and how awful a person I believed I had become since the memory resurfaced. I had nothing to lose and if it didn't work out, I could fall back on suicide. When I began to tell her, I wept. It occurred to me I had never said it out loud before to anyone but Perrine, and even then I didn't describe every detail. My words trembled as they fell from my mouth in broken syllables. I reached for the tissues sitting on Anne's desk and apologized for crying.

"You *never* have to apologize for crying." Her message wasn't a buddy mock-punching me in the arm. It was something she wanted me to absorb, accept, and understand. "Somewhere along the line, you were taught that it isn't okay to cry and I am telling you now that it is. It's a natural human response. If you feel you need to cry at any time, try not to stop yourself and tell yourself it's okay." Although I did accept what she was saying, I still felt like a cliché. I was sitting in a psychiatrist's office crying about my childhood. I suppose there's a reason that it's a cliché.

I made it through my story, and I glimpsed the tiniest hole in Anne's armor. I described how my eight-year-old self raced to hide the blood-soaked sheets from my mom. Anne's lips seemed to tighten ever so slightly. It may have been just an itch but I took it as a sign that she cared, which was important to me for reasons I had yet to understand.

Trying to lighten the mood, I pivoted the conversation to talk about my new love affair with Molly. It didn't seem to surprise her, and she asked if there were any other drugs I was taking. I assured her it was the only one and she, in her judgment-free fashion, told me to be careful with it and that we would discuss it again at our next session.

With the hour almost over, Anne looked me in the eyes and said, "I want you to know that it may get worse before it gets better. Your job is to hold on to the fact that it *will* get better." I didn't know what to say. *It gets worse?*

Why would she say that? Didn't I spend an hour telling her how much pain I was in and why? What in the actual fuck? I nodded my head and said nothing.

"And if you are feeling like you want to harm yourself, try to write down the catastrophic thoughts so we can discuss them. And if you feel like you might actually do something, please call me. You have my number."

After sessions with Anne, my body felt as though I had run a marathon. I'd make my way home where I would slide into bed and pass out into a deep sleep.

I saw Anne twice per week for a few months. Each time I would reveal and discover a new part of myself. I kept a promise to myself to be completely raw and honest with her even sharing my tendency to exaggerate and outright lie. I didn't want to lie anymore. I wanted to be comfortable with myself enough to not have to remember what lie I told to which person. Every time I lied, it was exhausting and I was almost always caught. We delved deeper into my budding addiction to MDMA, especially when I was able to mix it with sex.

"If you feel you absolutely need it when you are down, I don't see any harm if you're responsible about it. You just need to know why you want to take it," she said.

I assured her I would do it responsibly without really knowing what that meant. One pill? Three pills? Two pills and two girls? Two days in a row? Three? I experimented with all combinations to make sure. However, the problem was that if I were spiraling, I wouldn't take any. It would be on a random Wednesday night when the previous weekend's drugs were fading from my system and reality was setting back in. Reality was that I had to do my therapy homework which involved various readings, keeping a daily journal, and other activities. Anne also suggested I buy some LEGO and start watching *Star Wars* movies again so I could see the world through the eyes of that frightened little boy once more. These exercises prepared me for a more advanced, heart-wrenching task.

After some weeks of playing with LEGO blocks and watching the new *Star Wars Rebels* cartoon, Anne asked me to write letters to my eight-year-old self to tell him how he was worthy, how much he was loved, and that what happened to him was not his fault. I was to do this with my prominent right hand and respond as the eight-year-old with my weaker left hand. The exercise sent me plummeting into the depths of my psyche, shedding light on dark corners I'd neglected for more than thirty years. Not only did I have to step up and be strong for that eight-year-old, I had to *be* him again. I became the terrified, confused little boy who could not understand why someone would hurt him that way. A boy who couldn't process it to the point of hiding the memory away like those blood-stained sheets until an adult could deal with it. It was time. I was that adult—a forty-year-old, drug-addicted, sex-obsessed, binge alcoholic tourist.

Later, I realized that when Anne suggested that I "do drugs responsibly," she was planting the idea that I could do just that. She knew I'd consider her words when I was about to drop, which in itself was a small victory. It empowered me to govern myself in one tiny, but not so little, decision. Anne operated on a higher stratum than me.

As the wonderful world of Wednesdays continued to worsen, Perrine decided to visit. Our attempt at remaining friends fueled hope we might reconcile. I was still at work and I told her she could let herself into my house. She did and when I arrived home, she'd already left. On my desk lay my therapy journal. A place where I wrote my thoughts, my sins, the letters to the eight-year-old me. It was open on the page where I wrote down how guilty I felt about cheating on Perrine.

Though I'd been in love with Perrine, I was still unfaithful. I had many relationships and not once had I been loyal. I always had one foot out the door, never fully committed. I was never entirely "in" and even if I told myself I would be with Perrine, I wasn't. I continued my ongoing sexual relationship with a woman whom I'd started to sleep with during my first marriage. Our modus operandi was to go out for drinks with a group of friends and figure out a way to end up alone. Sometimes she met me at my office to have sex in a washroom, and we even sunk to the cliché of renting a cheap hotel room for an afternoon rendezvous. I'd also meet up with my dental hygienist who I'd started sleeping with when I was single. I began a new affair with a woman I'd met briefly at a party. I was trying to sink to the lowest bottom I could find. Sex was dirty and the only way to enjoy it was to keep it that way. Also, hurting the ones I loved most made it easier to hate myself and an effective way to destroy any happiness I knew I didn't deserve.

I was learning from Anne that the idea that I was unworthy began when I was eight years old, and I held onto this belief. I protected it and hid it from myself, and then it defined me. I created strategies to protect myself from being vulnerable. Embodying the asshole made it true.

Perrine called me later that night to ask the details of my infidelity. How many? Who were they? Had I used protection? Why? I assured her it was only one person, one time, and that I used protection. All outright lies. I described how it meant nothing and how it must have been because of the pain of what happened to me as a boy, shamelessly playing it like it was a get-out-of-jail-free card. I felt even worse for lying, and yet I continued. I didn't want to lose her entirely and was beginning to think that with therapy I could one day be capable of being with her again. She did nothing wrong. All she did was love me and try to help. Now, she was blindsided with learning that the person she loved so much cheated on her. Still, I believed she hoped we'd get back together, stronger for weathering the storm of this torment. She was delusional and so was I.

I didn't dwell on Perrine's unforgivable act of reading

my personal therapy journal and how, at a profoundly sensitive time in my therapy, she had broken my trust. I earned her distrust. As for the journal, it was no longer sacred. I destroyed it and with it, a vital branch of hope.

As the months wore on, Anne suggested that group therapy would be beneficial to me. I would be speaking with people who had suffered similar trauma, which could help assure all of us that we weren't alone. We could share coping strategies and give each other hope that we could recover. I hated the idea instantly. I had enough trouble telling one person in private, let alone a dozen strangers. I refused. "It's one strategy among many," she assured me, and we left it alone.

Two months into my therapy, on a Wednesday, I had an investors meeting where I was to present a summary of what my group, Engineering and Product, was doing and what we were planning to do in the future. I spent weeks preparing the presentation but botched it. My heart raced, I couldn't breathe, and I could barely finish my sentences. My partners stepped in to save me and finished the meeting while I sat in silence, humiliated and defeated. I had let them down and embarrassed us in front of investors, jeopardizing our company's future and their future. When the call was over, Mitchel didn't look at me as he left the room. Our normal protocol after these meetings was to debrief and run through what could have gone better. I said nothing and made my way back to my desk.

When I got home that night, I tossed my laptop bag on

the floor and made my way upstairs to my room. I sat at the top of my stairs and stared blankly at the wall. Logan greeted me and lay beside me. I replayed my failure over and over. I whispered, "It's OK, you're loved, just hang on." I was talking to the eight-year-old living inside the forty-year-old. The room blurred and I lay back to look at the ceiling. It was not melting. I was in the real world and it was painful. I wanted out. These are the catastrophic thoughts Anne was talking about. *Should I write these down?* I didn't move. I texted Perrine. She didn't answer. *I have a necktie ready with a noose in it.* The sound of tears hitting the floor beside my ears ticked like tiny taps.

I crawled over to my drug box and popped two Mollies. Anne said it was okay. I needed help and Molly was here for me. It was the first time I did Molly alone. I'd read somewhere that the hallmark of an alcoholic is if the person drinks alone. Is this a confirmation of my addiction? *Maybe I should call someone over.* But I didn't want anyone to see me like this. My body began to feel warm. The first wave was starting to hit me. I grabbed my laptop and opened it. I knew what to do.

My hands trembled as I pulled into the hotel parking lot. I wasn't sure if it was the Molly, which hit me hard, or how nervous I was. I parked the car and popped another one. Taking a deep breath, I picked up my phone. "I'm here," I typed.

"Room 412. Pay the girl when you arrive," was the response. The sun was setting behind the hotel building as I walked in. When the doors opened, the clerk looked over to me. I looked away and headed for the elevator. I wouldn't be checking in. Did he know why I was there? Was I about to be arrested? Should I abort this mission? My breath shortened and I stepped quickly into the elevator.

I knocked on the hotel room door. I heard footsteps approach and saw the light disappear from the peephole. The door opened to reveal a young woman in a white robe. She smiled and opened the door to let me in. I walked in, still nervous and high. "Hi," I said shyly.

"Hi," the woman giggled. "I'm Kay. Have a seat." Kay pointed at the bed and removed her robe. She wore a purple bra and yellow panties. Kay seemed genuinely happy when she smiled, an expression I didn't expect from a prostitute. I sat on the bed. I stared at her blankly while I calmed down. The pill I took downstairs wouldn't kick in for a while.

"Um, I just need to..." she started.

"Oh, right." I grabbed the amount I was told to bring and handed it to her. "How does tipping work? Should I do that now or...?" I asked as she counted the money.

"That's up to you, babe." Kay began typing on her phone. I decided to wait for the tip. When Kay was done with her phone, she made her way over to me. I lay back on the bed with my head on the pillow. "So, what are we going to do with our time?" she asked.

"I'm high," I blurted out. She looked into my eyes.

"On what, coke?"

"Molly." She laughed out loud.

"What a great idea for this kind of thing." She crawled into bed with me and laid her head on my chest. "I love Molly. Got any with you?"

"In the car I do." For a brief second I wondered if she was a cop and if I was about to be arrested for prostitution and drug possession.

"Darn," she said. "Next time, maybe. So, what would you like to do? I can do almost anything except anal." Her hands unbuckled my belt and she rubbed me from the outside.

"Actually, can we just hang out for a while?" Kay's hands stopped and she looked up at me. "I'm just working through some stuff."

"Sure, we can do anything you want, love." Kay wrapped her arm around my belly. I felt warm, loved, and not alone.

I asked Kay about her life and how she came to be doing what she was doing. She told me that she simply just loved sex, and most of the time it was easy money. She was from Montreal and came to Ottawa one or two days a week to make some money and then went back. I told her I'd spent a lot of time in Montreal throughout the years and we compared notes on favourite places like the Old Port and Saint Anne's in the West Island.

"Whoa, this third pill is kicking in," I told Kay, as a wave of warmth made its way up my body.

"Amazing, let's help that out." Kay pulled off my pants and moved down. Her hand slowly started to stroke my penis. I sighed in relief to feel that there was no erectile dysfunction from the Molly. It was all systems go. When I was leaving, Kay gave me a hug. "Hope everything works out."

"You, too." I walked back to my car. I preferred meeting Kay to writing down my catastrophic thoughts.

When I got back to my car, I saw my phone had a ton of messages, almost all of them from Perrine. "What's going on?" "Are you okay?" "Where are you?" I read through them all and responded.

"Hey, sorry, I wasn't near my phone. I'm okay. Was just feeling down."

"WTF. You can't just do that. Who are you with? Don't lie." I don't know why but I decided to be truthful with her and let the chips fall where they may.

"I was with a prostitute. I'm high." I hit send. I watched the "typing" notification turn on and off over the next few minutes with no message coming through.

"You're fucked," she finally typed back, the words staring up at me in judgmental disgust.

Broken

I WAS EIGHT YEARS OLD WHEN MY CHILDHOOD ENDED. Although I suppressed the memory of the rape, I became quiet and closed off. I pleaded with my mother to not leave me in bed alone. I told her I was afraid of monsters and she tried to quell my fears by employing a nightly ritual. Together, we'd conduct a thorough walkthrough of the bedroom, opening the closet door and pushing the hanging clothes to the side, then kneeling down to shine a light under the bed. This exercise calmed me down enough to get me in bed, but I still didn't feel safe. Mom had no choice but to leave me in bed alone to find my own way to fall asleep.

As soon as Mom was gone, I scanned the dark room in search of the monster. He was most likely under the bed, but I didn't trust the closet either. Each night I lay in fear staring at the ceiling until I was barely able to keep my eyes open. Eventually, fatigue forced my surrender and I accepted that I might die.

Joe was still around as he and Mom decided to reconcile their marriage. With the salon now gone and Joe laid off from his job, we took refuge in my grandparents' basement. French was my grandparents' first language, and they spoke it at home and encouraged me to do the same. My grandmother would sternly say "en Français" whenever I answered in English and she was speaking to me in French. Mom and even Joe were not above this rule.

My grandparents' house was a modest one-bedroom white bungalow on a corner facing a fenced-in soccer field. It had no garage, only a small backyard with a garden where they grew tomatoes, carrots, and radishes. In the basement was a semi-finished bedroom and washroom where Mom and Joe slept, leaving me to stay in a separate crevice next to the hot water tank and furnace. The furnace switched on and off as needed and when it ignited, it shot out a subtle wind-blast followed by a droning purr. The purr was soothing and helped me fall asleep. But if I wasn't asleep when the furnace turned off, the silence rang incessantly in my ears while I lay awake until the next cycle. My "room" was under a staircase, and the ceiling had exposed pipes and half-built walls. I slept on a used hospital bed that my grandfather procured from the hospital where he worked as a janitor. The staircase leading up to the main floor had no backing, leaving it exposed for anyone hiding under the stairs to grab your ankles. What seemed like a setting for a horror movie was now my bedroom. I diligently performed my nightly ritual of checking every possible place an intruder may be hiding. If I had to go to the bathroom, I would make sure I jumped far enough from the bed out of reach from potential hands grabbing at me, and dove back in upon my return. My other ritual of the acceptance of death continued as well. "If I'm going to die, then I'm going to die." I accepted my fate and shut my eyes.

The basement room was where my night terrors began. A court jester, his face painted like a clown, noticed me, eyeing me closely with a dark, satisfying grin. When I ran, he chased me with an ax. I ran as fast as I could, but running proved futile. A single blink later, I was back in the hospital bed in the boiler room. I lay paralyzed as the jester's ax thrust into my skull. The strike jolted me awake as I cried in terror. On one occasion, I darted out of the room, launching myself far from the bed and skipping as many steps on the exposed staircase as I could. I found myself alone in a dark kitchen. No one heard my cries. My heart pounded and my cheeks were cold, clammy from the tears. No one came and for some reason I didn't want them to. I found my way over to the sofa that sat against the wall of my grandparents' bedroom, curled up, and watched the streetlights shine through the darkness until morning.

I continued to have the dream about the jester. I continued to be afraid. I believed this was how people lived and that someday I'd get over the fear when I became an adult. But that fear bore itself deep into my psyche, rooting itself like crabgrass pushing its way into every crevice it could find. I was afraid of going to sleep, going to school, being alone, being with people, and going to the bathroom. Fear was now a part of my everyday life. Fear became its own being. Fear was my new father, my evil twin, my worst enemy. I faced him nightly and, as I grew up, I confronted him throughout the day too. He didn't speak. He didn't need to. He kept me in check and I started to need him. I needed him as much as he needed me. In my own way, I loved him. He reminded me that I was alive. He was the one reliable constant in my life. I gave him a name—Kevin.

Living with my grandparents was good for one big reason: my grandfather. When he saw me, he shuffled around the room excitedly, his slender body leaning to and fro while he reached out to take my hands to join in. I called him Grandpapa, which couldn't be said without a French accent like the thick one he had. An avid hockey fan, my grandfather and I watched games together. We'd bet on the outcome. He would purposely pick who he thought would lose, letting me win whenever I could. I couldn't wait for Saturday because it meant *Hockey Night in Canada*. We taunted and trash talked about who was going to win. Every time my team scored, I ran around the house shouting, announcing how I would be spending the fifty cents I was about to collect.

Years later, my mother recounted a story about Grandpapa to me. Grandpapa was in the kitchen fixing himself some tea. In my excitement I ran over to him as fast as I could and grabbed onto him. The burning hot water spilled over his leg, scalding his skin. He didn't scream or say anything. I can only imagine how much pain he was in as he calmly set the cup back on the counter, handed me to my mother, and retreated to the washroom to survey the damage. He lost a layer of skin, resulting in a permanent scar. He never said a word to me, but my Mom and grandmother warned me to be careful in the kitchen. Not too long after that day, my grandfather had a heart attack and died. The night he died, my grandmother came home from the hospital and found me on the sofa. She hugged me, sobbing with her face in my hand. I didn't completely understand that I would never see Grandpapa again, but I cried along with my grandmother as she soaked the palm of my hand with her tears.

At my grandmother's urging and her devotion to retain our heritage, Mom enrolled me in a French elementary school, Ecole Notre Dame. Notre Dame forbade students from speaking English on school grounds, a rule to which I seldom complied. After the rape, my grades fell dramatically. Comments in my report cards went from words like "bright, attentive, friendly" to "daydreams in class, not applying himself, lazy."

One day I found myself in the principal's office. I don't remember why, because it happened so frequently. I trembled as I sat across from him at his desk. When he spoke, I heard only distant vowel sounds until one word he uttered made its way to me loud and clear—spanking. I must've done something egregious enough to warrant corporal punishment. Up until now, I had gotten used to the ruler whippings administered by the teachers themselves. A ruler whipping was when I had to hold out my hand palm up while the teacher slapped it with a ruler several times. There was a rumour among the students that if we were to lick our palms before the whipping, your hand would bleed and the teacher would get in trouble. I was never brave enough to try it.

After telling me that I was going to be spanked, the principal called another man into the room. I had not seen this man before and he didn't look like he was a teacher at the school. The principal took me by the arm and made me stand in the middle of the room while the other man watched. Instead of instructing me to hold out my hand, he told me to pull down my pants. My trembling worsened. I pulled them down and he insisted the underwear come down as well. Terrified, I complied. He had me bend over and he felt my backside with his hand, then slapped it. Hard. Sharp, white pain pulsed through my body. I whimpered, but quietly. My mind tried to make sense of what was happening. These were two adults and I was a bad boy, so I accepted that this is how bad boys were punished. Still, it didn't seem right and I couldn't understand why. He continued to spank me barehanded. When he finished, I pulled up my clothes and hobbled out. I told Mom, but she sided with the principal. "Maybe you shouldn't have been bad," she said. The experience pushed me further into introversion and social anxiety. The memory of office spanking festered. Years escaped me while overwhelming fear and painful solitude intensified. In any interaction with adults other than my mother, I would not speak. As a preteen, I was bullied daily, and a part of me blamed the principal. I needed for him to pay. For everything. When I was fourteen and felt strong enough, I decided how.

I left school one lunch hour. I took a city bus to my old school with a steak knife in my pocket. My body shook from adrenaline, not unlike the trembling I felt that day in his office. On the bus that afternoon, my mind held visions of police crouched behind their open car doors, their guns aimed at me as I walked out of the front doors of the school, bloody knife in hand. The scene that played out in my mind was not a deterrent; rather it was a welcomed relief, an assumed finality that I'd be taken away.

I walked through the front doors to the school office and asked to see the principal. The secretary paused, visibly distressed at my question. I explained that I was a former student and that I wanted to say hi. Taking a breath, she apologized and informed me that he had died. *He was fucking dead already.* My shaken lack of response was for a much different reason than she thought, but it must have resembled how a person might react to sad news. I stumbled out of the school to nothing: no police cars, no flashing lights, no crowds of people to gawk and point in horror. I was alone. I had no purpose and since I wasn't leaving in handcuffs, I had to make my way home. I showed up at home later than usual to a moderately angry mother who asked where I was and why I'd cut class. My traditional "I don't know" answer was met with a grounding for an undisclosed and unmonitored time.

One year after my father and his wife, Carol, had Michelle, my mother and Joe had a baby girl, Natalie. Aside from summer visits and Christmases, I didn't get to know Michelle until my later years; I lived with Natalie while she grew up. Given Mom's new responsibility of raising another child, I was left even more to my own devices. In school, I was a daydreamer who found it hard to focus. Looking over old transcripts, a coterie of teachers from the many different schools described me using the same words. "He has potential but does not apply himself," or "Rob does not pay attention in class." They were all right, of course.

Throughout my early teens, a trickle of girls appeared for whom I had vague feelings. Painfully awkward moments of wondering if a kiss on the cheek or the lips was the correct action to take. More frequently than not, I opted for the cheek, figuring as a good starting point. I was not yet cautioned about the perils of the friend zone. These events never escalated, and the excitement of the new fell into the depths of boredom. It was up to me to try to push it to the next level even though I had no idea what the next level was. There was no white whale called sex.

I was still too afraid of it. My curiosity about sex was the same as my curiosity about what it would be like to pet a great white shark. It'd be cool to tell my friends about it, but I may lose my arm.

When I liked a girl, I bored her with endless phone conversations praying there would be kissing in the foreseeable future. I loved kissing. It was a way to be close and intimate beyond the limitations of friendship, yet without the severe threat of what I feared sex was going to be. I liked being what I thought was innocent, while sex seemed dirty. Not having sex also meant I wouldn't be discovered as someone who had no idea what he was doing. I could have navigated these waters far better had I just been honest. I could have told them I was afraid. I could have said to them that I didn't know why. I could have told them I wanted to wait. Instead, I planted seeds in their minds that made them think I had a lot of experience. I discovered how to manipulate through not speaking. I insisted that I wouldn't reveal what I had done in the sexual arena, as it would dishonour my previous partners and the experience itself. Unfortunately, my respectful silence only made them curious and wanting me more, which was not what I wanted. What I wanted was too narrow a goal. I wanted the girls to believe I was experienced and desire me, yet keep me at an arm's length and not push for the things I was not ready to do.

By the time I was fifteen, I became too much for my Mom to handle. Joe was out of the picture and Mom had no help taking care of a rebellious teenage boy and a five-year-old girl. I began shoplifting, something I turned out to be terrible at given that I was caught every time. One of these adventures led to the store calling the police. Fortunately, it was only a tactic to scare me straight. The effects didn't last and Mom knew it. I was also getting into fights at school which were not two-way altercations. It was me getting hit a lot and coming home bloody—once with a broken jaw, resulting in my jaw being wired shut for weeks. While flying through the turbulence of dealing with a problem teen, Mom wanted to restart her life. It was an idea that seemed to emerge annually, but this time she wanted to restart it on the other side of the country in Kelowna, British Columbia. Mom reached out to my father and I was shipped off to Dad's home in Montreal for my high school years.

Don't Call it Frisco

I HATE THE COLD. OTTAWA IS A PLACE WHERE THE AIR hurts your skin in the winter. Even though therapy was providing a tiny sliver of hope, I decided to escape it and winter in San Francisco. When I told Perrine that I was going to leave the city for a few months, she was surprisingly supportive. My last night in town, Perrine came over to watch the series finale of *Dexter* and to say goodbye.

Anne was disappointed I was leaving. We were making good progress and she was concerned that I may not be stable enough to be without a support network. She had a good point. She had many good points but I was going anyway. Anne reintroduced the group therapy idea and gave me a list of meetings she found in San Francisco that she had researched for me. I considered it a bit more this time. I'd be in a different city with no possibility of anyone knowing me. I could truly be anonymous. A few days after I arrived, I looked at the list and did some research of my own. I decided I'd participate in an online group to see how it went before attempting an in-person meeting as Anne suggested.

The meeting was a group chat with anyone from any city, all with anonymous handles. A moderator explained the rules about privacy, respect, and a bit about the technical side. I hadn't considered the administrative challenges of not being in the same room. Anyone could sign in and type anything to anyone. And that's what happened. Soon after the moderator typed out the rules one of the participants started ranting, "This is so fucking stupid." The moderator asked him to leave, but to no avail. I let them go at each other for a few minutes, then walked away from the screen for a drink. I figured the other participants did the same. When I returned, it was still going on and I turned off the computer, thus ending my group therapy experience.

I didn't settle for staying in a humble apartment in San Francisco. I found a beautiful loft penthouse in a historic building not unlike my own in Ottawa. I was still trying to find happiness in my surroundings rather than looking inward. The loft was in the trendy South of Market, or SoMa, neighborhood, and owned by a well-known interior designer named David. Upon arriving, David met me and escorted me to the loft. David was flamboyantly gay and very friendly. He asked me about my visit, and I explained that I was there alone to work and to enjoy the city.

I had one friend in San Francisco, Sean. Sean had a

startup like one of mine, and we had met through my reaching out to see if there could be any synergy between our two companies. There didn't turn out to be any, but through emails and conference calls, we became friends. When I mentioned I would be in SF for a while, he quickly invited me to a party he was hosting. It turned out to be the first night I arrived in the city.

After unloading my luggage into the loft, I got into a cab and found my way there. The small party Sean mentioned was not a small party at all. He sold his company and purchased a mansion for his fraternity and the party was the celebration. There were games rooms, multi-level concrete patios, and large-screen TVs playing videos of women in mermaid costumes swimming underwater. This wasn't a frat party, however. There were investors, and his family there as well. "Rob!" Sean yelled from across the room. I smiled and waved while simultaneously feeling the heat from my embarrassment as everyone looked at me wondering who I was.

"Hey brother," Sean hugged me with one arm as he held his drink in another. "Sick place. I'm so glad you made it! You got in today, right?"

"Yeah, long day. Frisco is gorgeous," I snickered uncomfortably.

"Awesome. Listen, I have to shmooze with my new bosses and team for a bit. Help yourself to anything and we'll chat later." Sean had far more important people to talk to.

"Sounds good, man, thanks. Oh, and congrats on the sale."

"Ha-ha, thanks. Hey, if you don't want to sound like a tourist, don't call it Frisco. It's San Francisco or SF."

"Good tip," I laughed and Sean stepped into another conversation. I was left to my own devices. I had a few drinks while I awkwardly strolled through the house. I wasn't the best at introducing myself to strangers and this was my first time in California, but it didn't take long for someone to relieve the anxiety.

Kim, a scientist studying at Stanford, was soft-spoken, highly intelligent and came across a little shy. I felt she was as tipsy as I was. She felt sorry for me when she saw me walking around alone, so she walked up and introduced herself. Kim had a quick dry wit that I failed miserably at trying to emulate which, thankfully, made me more endearing. We continued to drink and she gave me her number. We went out a couple of times for dinner and, although I didn't feel any connection, we had wonderful discourse. I felt smarter whenever we spent time together. On our second date, I mentioned I love raving and that I might hop over to Reno to catch Avicii. Kim loved that I was so spontaneous and wanted to join me. Why not, I figured, and we booked our flight.

We agreed to stay in the same room but didn't discuss it. I had no expectations either way. I hadn't brought up the topic of drugs but it wasn't as if I had any, or had any sources, anyway. It's not as if I would try and buy some from a perfect stranger in Reno. I could just go and enjoy the music, right?

When we got to the rave in Reno and the music started, all I wanted was the accompanying high. It took me about five and a half seconds to see a group handing pills to each other. I made my way over to them and the one handing them out looked at me suspiciously. I mouthed, "Can I buy some?" while showing him the cash in my hand. He smirked as he thoroughly looked around while walking over. He asked how many. I figured that all I needed was one but that I may want two and so might Kim, and it's always handy to have an extra just in case. *Drug math.* "Six," I answered. He told me the extortionate price, I gave him the money, and he handed me a tiny bag with the capsules. It looked like he had a bunch of pre-filled tiny bags for people like me. I took his number in case I needed more.

Kim let me know she had no interest in drugs, but she didn't dissuade me from doing any. I assured her the pills would only make me dance around like an excited toddler, but other than that she would barely notice. By the end of the night, Kim was still dancing with me and smiling, and it at least looked like she was having fun. I downed a second pill and we decided to go back to the hotel to drink whatever was in the minibar. When we got back Kim jumped on me and started kissing me. My mind was not in a sexual space but it raced there quickly. Surprised at her aggression, I reciprocated. I offered her a pill and she decided to take a half. *That's how it starts*, I thought. For a split second I wondered if offering a drunk woman I barely knew some drugs might be starting something that could become a problem. But I was too out of my head to stay with any thought very long, let alone balancing ethical dilemmas, especially as I was about to have sex with someone new. Kim's high kicked in incredibly fast and powerfully. We were already having sex and her moans increased in frequency and intensity. Her eyes looked at me puzzled and excited. "Is this how it always feels?"

"Yes!" I gave her some water and told her we had to keep drinking it. Her inhibitions melted away and she jumped around asking to try different positions. It reminded me of my first sexual experience while high. We had sex for hours and passed out in a sweaty cuddle.

Kim and I parted ways at the airport in San Francisco. We never saw each other again. We each had our reasons. Kim had better things to do with her time than to spend it with an addict, and I wasn't willing to give up being one.

The owner of my rented loft, David, had an assistant, Danielle. Danielle was a grad student in her last year at a prestigious design school. Danielle possessed an undeniable presence, and I watched her closely as she entered the room. I wasn't necessarily attracted to her, but I instantly liked everything about her. She asked if I would like to be shown around the town and we decided to have dinner together. Neither of us considered it a date. I was in no position to try dating someone, and Danielle wasn't interested in getting into anything until she finished school.

We shared laughs over countless glasses of wine in one of San Francisco's many incredible sushi restaurants. The knowledge that our time together was without any romantic undercurrent provided a reassurance that propelled my confidence. When the night was over, we hugged awkwardly. If it were a high five, we would've missed. Mutually embarrassed, we went our separate ways agreeing to do it again soon. A week later, we went to dinner and the mood changed. As she sipped her red wine, I studied her full red lips and voluminous dark hair. I started to wonder what it would be like to see Danielle romantically. The fact remained that I was not in any shape to start a relationship. This didn't stop me of course. Maybe it would be good for me, I reasoned. Maybe it would help me get my shit together and act like a grown-up.

We flirted more and began falling in love. Danielle was reluctant, however. I was only planning on being in San Francisco for a couple of months and a long-distance relationship was out of the question for her. I wish I could have been respectful enough to leave it at that and just remain friends, but I didn't. I was still the selfish asshole I'd always been, and I wanted what I couldn't have even more. I told her I would consider moving to San Francisco permanently, even though I had no idea how it would work. We kept seeing each other and fell deeper in love.

Danielle took me to a speakeasy, a "secret" bar for which San Francisco was known. It operated unsubtly hidden behind a bookshelf door in the back of a dive bar. Customers with half-grown beards, zip hoodies, and jeans draped over running shoes or loafers filled the speakeasy. The male bartender appeared to know Danielle and flirted with her heavily. He sported a handsome, tight-fitting vest in the fashion of the time of the speakeasies. He and I seemed to play some sort of game. Every time Danielle and I ordered a new cocktail, he would make sure mine was overwhelmingly feminine by serving them in dainty glasses decorated with flowers and mini-umbrellas. Danielle and I caught on, and each time we laughed more. The bartender's antics backfired. Laughing at my feminine drinks only served to bring us closer.

Round after round, our conversation became more personal. Somehow, we broached the topic of drugs. Danielle said she liked to do weed occasionally, especially after she'd been on Molly the night before. *Wait, what?* Danielle, the gorgeous, intelligent, stay-in-school-type did drugs? *My* drug? My body jolted in excitement. All I could think of from that moment on was how to score some Molly and get high with Danielle. I played it nonchalant and told her I had also done Molly before and that maybe we should try it together sometime. No pressure.

The following weekend we decided to go to a club and take a couple of pills. We popped together and I discreetly took two when Danielle took one. When the night was over, we went back to my place and ripped off each other's clothes. Our genuine connection was amplified by the Molly, not manufactured by it. In the morning, I woke up to an empty bed. Danielle had slipped out. Alone and embarrassed, I lay in bed, again battling the depressive recovery alone. I did it again. I used drugs to get closer to someone I really liked in some sort of contrived manipulation. Did she even like me at all or was it the drugs? I had no idea. I decided to never see her again. She was way out of my league anyway, and being with me would only bring her down. I'd probably ruin her life, just as I felt I'd ruined Perrine's. No one deserves that.

Danielle texted me the next evening. She'd had fun and, contrary to my plan, I found myself asking if she wanted to hang out the following weekend. We dropped Molly again. We continued the roller-coaster ride for weeks. We would pop on a Thursday and Danielle would "work from home" on Friday to recover. Or we'd do it on a Friday, leaving us the weekend to recuperate in bed with delivered food. One weekend we decided to drive down the coast. I rented a bright red convertible Ferrari and we were off. We took the famous Highway 1 down to the Ritz Carlton in Half Moon Bay. I rented us a suite on the Gold level, meaning it included unlimited booze in their lounge. When we got there, we each popped a pill and started drinking in the lounge. The more we stayed in the lounge, the more we felt out of place. We decided to explore the resort and found ourselves in a back area that had a large outdoor fire-table and what looked like a makeshift bar. We tossed our jackets on a couple of chairs by the fire, and headed to the bar. This wasn't an ordinary bar. It offered a variety of flavoured and liqueured hot chocolates. We were in heaven. Normally the thought of eating food on Molly is repugnant, but there are a few exceptions. Sweet drinks, fruit, and chocolate. Danielle and I drank more and took more Molly until we were puddles on the floor of our hotel room.

Danielle lay on her back with her hands above her head. She smiled at the ceiling and stretched out her body with a relieving sigh. I climbed over to her gently. I lifted her white blouse to reveal her belly button. Her hands came down cautiously, ready to stop any potential tickling attempt. I kissed her stomach. "I was thinking," I said as I kissed her again. "Do you wanna be, you know, exclusive?" I looked up to see her smile. My hand softly caressed her skin.

"You asking me to be your girlfriend?" Danielle stretched her body again and closed her eyes.

"I am."

"I like that idea." She motioned me closer with her finger without opening her eyes. I obeyed.

We became a couple, high. Perfect.

The next few weeks continued with much of the same. Danielle would work while finishing her course, and I was working on the new business. Every weekend consisted of discovering a new trendy restaurant that Danielle would know about, followed by drinks, drugs and recovery. I went home to Ottawa for a few weeks, but returned to SF to continue our spiral. I was still talking to Perrine, and when I told her I was seeing someone new she became livid. Perrine found Danielle on Facebook and wrote her a long email warning her about my recovery from rape, my marital indiscretions, and how I had recently been with a prostitute. Danielle forwarded me the email and asked if it was true. I had already told Danielle I was in therapy recovering from a childhood trauma, so that didn't surprise her. But, understandably, she was concerned that I was with a prostitute and that she may have been exposed to a sexually transmitted disease. I assured her it was just a "crazy ex" that had a vendetta and there was nothing to worry about.

I had done this most of my life. Even when I was caught red-handed, I would deny it was true. If a girlfriend were to walk in a room to find me inside another woman, I would deny it was happening. I suffered from some sort of delusion that prevented me from simply admitting to what I had done, because to do so would mean that there was a reason for it and I was too afraid to look into that frightening dark corner of myself. And because of that fear I hurt people. Good people. People who loved me.

My relationship with Danielle was more aspirational than actual. Not so deep down, I knew I didn't deserve to be with her. I don't mean in a pathetic I-don't-deserve-anyone kind of way. I simply wasn't able to reciprocate the depth of love she offered. What's worse is that I didn't tell her. I went on as if I was going to move to a new city for her so that we could be together. I had no real plans to move, however. After the initial few months, I only returned twice.

* * *

Back home, Mitchel was working on our charity boxing event called Fight for the Cure, in which white-collar Canadian celebrities get in the ring to fight. With little to no experience, the competitors trained for a few months to prepare and then, at a black-tie gala, competed in a sanctioned amateur, Olympic-style boxing bout. Proceeds went to our local Cancer Foundation and the city ate it up. We charged thousands of dollars for a table that included a dinner and real amateur bouts along with the white-collar fights. The event quickly became a must-attend on the city's elite social calendars.

While I was in San Francisco, a Liberal politician from Montreal had heard about our event and was interested. His name was Justin Trudeau, son of Pierre Trudeau, one of Canada's most popular prime ministers. We managed to find an opponent for Justin in a Conservative senator, Patrick Brazeau. Patrick was a controversial representative from the First Nations and although he looked professional in a suit, he looked more like a henchman when he wore his workout gear. He was stocky, muscular, and covered in tribal tattoos. Justin was the poster boy of the country with his iconic thick, dark hair that reached his shoulders. He was younger looking than his age of forty. He was tall, slender, and spoke with great charm and wit. Trudeau and Brazeau had open arguments in the House of Commons and shot insults over Twitter, which hyped up the gala.

I'd played a bigger role in organizing Fight for the Cure with Mitchel in previous years, but my ongoing self-destruction and truancy limited my contribution. I flew back to Ottawa from San Francisco only weeks before the event when most of the work was already done.

On the night of the gala, the entire country and the entire world watched. Politicians from opposite sides of the aisle were stepping in the ring to fight it out and the media ate it up. Chowen even flew in for the big night, as did Danielle. At one point, I introduced Danielle as Perrine to a friend. As soon as Perrine's name came out of my mouth, I was mortified. Although Danielle didn't let it show, I'm certain she was too. The moment we were alone, I apologized profusely. Danielle assured me it was fine and that things like this happened. I kissed her. Minutes later I was asked to do a live interview on one of the networks. Fortunately, I was completely sober and made it through the interview without any trouble.

The night played out like a movie. The bigger, stronger Brazeau came out swinging. He tried to knock out

Trudeau and came close to doing so, but Trudeau waited him out, just like Muhammad Ali's Rope-A-Dope strategy when he fought George Foreman. By the third round Brazeau was so tired he couldn't lift his hands up to protect himself. Trudeau took full advantage, hammering away with head and body shots. The referee stopped the fight and Trudeau won the bout by a Technical Knockout or TKO. The gala, and the bout win, served as a catalyst that propelled Trudeau to becoming the leader of his party and, not too long after, Canada's prime minister. Brazeau's career went a different way. After a series of arrests involving domestic abuse and other violations, he went from being a tenured Conservative senator to manager of a local strip club.

I stayed sober for the entire event but had plans to go out afterwards. As soon as the gala was over Chowen, Danielle, and I popped some Molly and jumped into a limo that took us to my favourite nightclub. "Saw the event on TV. I'm so proud of you man!" said Branson as he brought me in for a hug. I thanked him. "Rob, this is Deadmau5." I looked over to see the famous EDM DJ and shook his hand. I didn't recognize him as Deadmau5 wears an iconic giant mouse head when he performs.

"Wow, so cool to meet you." I smiled. Chowen positioned us to take a photo together.

"I heard you raised a shit-ton of money for charity tonight, man. Congrats," said Deadmau5 while he overemphasized a smile not unlike a toddler posing for the picture. Right then an enormous drug wave hit me. I realized that I hadn't eaten as I was at the venue all day preparing for the event. It blurred my vision, rocked my knees, and slurred my speech. Deadmau5 felt me lean back. I turned to him and mumbled something indecipherable. "Whoa, you're fucked up, eh?" I smiled and he laughed. So much for discretion.

After regaining a semblance of composure, I had a drink followed quickly by another, and another. The next thing I remember was waking up at home on my washroom floor. A path of vomit led from where I had passed out, up the side of the toilet bowl, into the water. While I observed the puke path, its odor wafted subtly into my sinuses triggering another, now sober and conscious, stomach evacuation. I jumped at the bowl and forced out a few ounces of bile. Even after a few small heaves, I felt a little better. I made my way to the shower, but not before a visit with my toothbrush, and cleaned myself off. I joined Danielle in bed. She was still sleeping, so I passed out beside her. Danielle and I spent the next forty-eight hours on my couch watching movies and ordering junk food after which I drove her to the airport for her flight home.

Two weeks later, I broke up with Danielle over the phone. It was clear that I couldn't move to San Francisco, and Danielle did not want a long-distance relationship. If I wanted it bad enough, I could have made it work, but I didn't. I didn't just leave Danielle. I left the person I could have been.

A week after the breakup, I tried to commit suicide in my condo while thinking about passwords. I failed and crushed my windpipe instead. I couldn't speak for days, but my resolve to die solidified. I'd clearly been subconsciously trying to die in my drug abuse and alcoholism. It was time to do it consciously.

Accelerate

AS I LAY IN MY OWN BILE ON THE FLOOR, LOGAN CAME over to headbutt me affectionately. I struggled to breathe, unable to make a sound other than a faint wheezing. I lay there and wept. When I was able to, I slowly, dizzily sat up. I pet the cat. Add another item to the list: someone to take care of Logan when I'm gone. This was not a call for attention. It was just a matter of time before I would execute the task successfully. Up until that point in my life, I had saved a decent amount of money in some fantastical, misguided notion of retirement or whatever abstract idea I had around it. Given the decision to die, I decided to spend as much of the "nest egg" as I could. Being alone, depressed, *and* without money would provide an added incentive and may help me finish the job.

While sober, the anxiety I felt from work eclipsed the pain from my personal life. If there was any time when I was sober and felt the shock of my trauma, I turned to work. It filled the lonely nights as I toiled away on my laptop in my dark living room surrounded by half-eaten junk food and with Logan perched nearby. Kevin liked it this way and continued to encourage me to avoid the pain at all costs. I would show him, though. Once I'm gone, he'd be gone.

The life goal now was to go out in a Leaving-Las-Vegas-esque train wreck and I knew just the way to do it. I had to step up my drug use. I asked my drug dealer if I could buy larger quantities. She introduced me to her supplier, Luc. Luc was good looking, young and fit, but came across very differently from what I envisioned a drug dealer to be. He had a heavy French-Canadian accent and was incredibly warm and friendly. Luc was, however, able to turn unfriendly very quickly if he felt he needed to intimidate someone, something I'd witness often as our friendship evolved. When I met him, I didn't want to beat around the bush so I told him outright that I hated running out of Molly and that I wanted to buy a lot for my own use. He suggested that I buy in crystal form and that I could "cap it" myself. Capping meant that I would have to crush the crystals of Molly into a fine enough powder in order to fill an empty capsule. I had no idea what he was talking about, but shrugged my shoulders in agreement.

Luc said he could get me an ounce and see if that would last me. It turns out an ounce was a lot even for me. It was about one hundred and thirty-five pills if I dosed correctly, which I didn't. I had no idea what I was doing and far too embarrassed to ask. I didn't even bother

Googling how. I bought the ounce and ordered capsules online. The capsules were way too big and I filled them much more than I should have. A recommended dose of MDMA is 0.1 grams. I filled the capsules with 0.3 to 0.5 grams. I would take one of these pills when I was out, and with the first wave my body would become immersed in a snug embrace of thick, warm air while my knees would buckle as if someone kicked them from behind. Next my jaw would oscillate from clenching tightly to an inability to form words. Anyone who was with me would ask what was wrong. Discretion had fallen to the wayside. I tried to convince myself that I was hiding my drug use well. I wasn't. I realized that the doses were too high but instead of doing what any rational human being would do, like cut back the dosage, I decided I needed a better place to be high. It wasn't a drug problem; it was a geographic challenge.

The local scene in Ottawa lacked the intensity, and anonymity, that Vegas offered. Moreover, every weekend the same people surrounded me. People who, if they looked close enough, might recognize that I had a problem if they hadn't already. People who might try to stop me, or worse, try to help me. I needed to branch out and find a place where I could let go and not worry about onlookers who would judge me. I learned about an all weekend event called the Osheaga Music and Arts Festival, also held in Montreal. The event had a different vibe. Osheaga was held outside during the day and into the evening. A group of people I knew invited me to join. I was hesitant but after learning that they too enjoyed their drugs, I was in.

When we arrived in the midafternoon, food trucks, booze tents, and kiosks selling memorabilia lined up from the entrance all the way to the audience. Hip-hop pounded through the loudspeakers that stood on twenty-foot-tall scaffolding. The moment we got in, one of our crew bought us all a round of beers and told everyone to chug it. "Let's get the day started off right!" he yelled. I popped my first pill of Molly and chased it with the beer. After polishing it off quickly, he looked at me and smiled. "I put two in yours," he said, winking. *Fuck.*

"I just used it to chase my first." I wasn't sure he could hear me over the music.

"I guess you're starting with three then, my friend." He laughed and hit the back of my shoulder. I laughed with him and prepared myself for the high to come.

The sunny, upbeat music festival suddenly became a dark rhythmic tribal dance. Eminem hit the stage and his voice emanated pure anger. I'd enjoyed Eminem's music for years but the Molly put me in a vulnerable state and now his voice was offending me, as if he were attacking me. I had no idea why I would like someone who said the things he said. In my confusion, I found myself alone in the crowd. I lost everyone I was with. I began to hyper-ventilate. I was in a dense sea of fist-pumping, seemingly pissed off hip-hop fans. I worked my way through the crowd, feeling every touch of sweaty concertgoers, occasionally finding myself immersed in thick clouds of weed smoke. I inhaled deeply. It made it worse. When I finally emerged, I leaned up against a railing. I stood still until I was able to figure out where I should go.

Holding the railing tightly, I ignored the lyrics and focused on the vibrations of the bass. I bobbed my head in unison. The wave subsided and I felt my legs again. Somehow Kaylee, a friend that was part of the crew I was with, found me and brought me back to the group. We danced for hours. I took a pill of speed to prevent me from getting tired and more Molly to keep the high. When it was midnight, the music stopped. The instant silence struck me. When you're rolling on Molly and the music stops, your mind searches for more as if the ground were missing and your legs straddled the air. We looked at each other bewildered, but Kaylee had a plan. There was an after-hours club called Underground where we could go. The rest of the group shied away and said they were calling it a night. Apparently not everyone, or anyone, was as high as I was. Kaylee rallied and recruited another friend to join.

In a pre-Uber era, it was impossible to find a cab at that time and somehow the three of us ended up on a city bus. The city bus took us downtown and we were able to walk the rest of the way to Underground. We were searched thoroughly before we were able to enter. I wasn't worried this time. I had no drugs left to hide.

When you first walk into Underground, all you can see through the thick haze of smoke is a few red lights. There were two separate areas, each with their own music, bars, and dance floor. The bars did not sell alcohol, however. After-hour clubs like Underground couldn't sell alcohol outside of the legally-defined hours. Instead they charged unreasonable cover charges, and sold Red Bull, Gatorade, and water. The washroom was close to the entrance, and I made my way to it. There was a short stocky man with thick glasses standing against the wall between the washrooms. He looked directly at me. "Need anything?" he asked. I was surprised at how out in the open he was.

"What do you have?" We were surrounded by a cloud of smoke, not from cigarettes but from a machine that kept the bar doused in murkiness. I felt the bass through the walls.

"Are you a cop?" he asked. I assumed I would legally have to say if I was a cop if all those cop-dramas were true.

"No." I looked at him in his eyes to mark my sincerity.

"Ecstasy, coke, speed," he said in a thick French accent.

"Do you have Molly?"

"No. Ecstasy, coke and speed."

"Okay, I'll have an Ecstasy," I said. He turned and motioned for me to follow him.

He led me into a washroom stall. "Twenty," he said. I wasn't in any position to bargain. He was clearly a part of the club, which meant that all the security was a part of it too. I paid him and he pulled out his stash, which was a big clear bag full of smaller baggies. He reached in and took out a blue pressed pill not unlike the pills I took in Vegas.

"Merci," I said and we left the stall. I swallowed the pill. The bitter chalk caught in my throat. Drinking water didn't help. I convinced myself that they probably relied heavily on repeat business, so it wouldn't be in their best interest to poison their clientele. I calmed down when I remembered that I no longer cared. I wasn't in the business of living.

When I rejoined the girls, we walked down a corridor and past the first bar that overlooked the central dance floor. The sound pierced through my temples into my chest. A dark, throbbing, rhythmic beat of deep house music reverberated through my body. Dozens of souls gyrating, spinning, half-fist-pumping to the heart-thumping bass pulsating through the air. Most of the men wore no shirt, women barely wore bras, others leaned against the walls with their eyes rolled back in their heads nodding in failed unison. Small groups of seemingly sober concertgoers huddled together close to their tribes, but this was clearly a drug lair and we were not welcome. It was their home, their safe place out of sight of judging eyes. My eyes were not judging, however. My eyes were envious. I wanted into this world. I joined the crowd and started to dance. The stage blew more smoke into the crowd and we could barely see in front of us. I connected to the music and everyone in the room. I lost myself in the dank, shadowy, melodic air. I had no idea where the girls went. It didn't matter. This hell was my new heaven.

Kaylee interrupted my swaying stupor and yanked me into a backroom into which she and her friend were invited. She handed me a bottle of water and ordered me not to wander off. The backroom was a beautiful spacious lounge with large sofas and high ceilings, and we were the only people there. Kaylee's friend, a tall well-dressed man, came around the corner with drinks for us all. The drinks made the girls uncomfortable, so they didn't drink them. Neither did I. I sat there while they chatted but my mind was still on that dance floor with my new coterie of compatriots. I didn't get a chance to rejoin them. Kaylee felt too uncomfortable to stay. She likely didn't want to babysit me anymore. We made our way back to our hotel and once again I found myself in bed staring at my beloved melting ceilings.

Kaylee and I began going out every weekend. I popped pills of Molly while we were out to enhance my own high. After a few weeks of spending a lot of time together, we started to have sex. I kept to my radical honesty promise, making it abundantly clear that we would not be entering a relationship, and I told her when I was with other women. I didn't want to be cruel, but I also didn't want to give her hope that our relationship would become more than just friendship with sex. We fell into a routine of going out, getting drunk and high, having sex and me leaving quickly in the morning. Other nights I did the same with other girls. In the moments when we were alone, the Molly helped me feel and act as if I were connected to them. When this happened, they would begin to feel like what we had was more than sex, which invariably led to a "where-is-this-going?" conversation, which in turn led to a goodbye. There was nothing wrong with any of these women. In fact, every one of them meant something to me or I wouldn't have gotten close to them to begin with. I was the one who was fucked up. I was the one who was wrong. None of these women deserved me as I was, and none of them deserved how I was with them. I was on my way out and soon they would understand.

Sandstorm

WEEKS WENT BY AS I ESCALATED MY DRUG USE. IT NO longer mattered what city I was in. I'd meet Chowen in Vegas whenever I could, escape to Montreal if someone was willing to take the drive, hit up one of Branson's clubs, or I'd simply stay home and get high with whatever girl I could coax to come over. During the week, I worked every waking, recovering hour. On weekends, I was just as diligent in my consistency in avoiding being sober. During one of our Vegas binges, Chowen suggested we go to a rave he heard about called Electric Daisy Carnival or EDC Las Vegas.

When I researched it online, I came across trailer videos on YouTube. I couldn't take my eyes off the screen. Beautiful women donned in sparkly outfits and with glitter on their exposed bodies jumped in the warm night air. Their eyes completely closed, they soaked up the sound while flaunting a meditative Buddhist smile. This was their nirvana, and I wanted to be enlightened. But more importantly, this was my chance. I could load up on as many drugs as I could get my hands on and peak at the most opportune moment. If I did it right, I could overdose at the height of my high. I could find peace surrounded by a hundred thousand of my closest friends.

I had been so busy working or being high, I did none of the things I told myself I was going to do before leaving the world. I said goodbye to no one. I made no arrangements. I wrote down no passwords. I considered no one else's inconvenience, or feelings, but my own. It didn't matter. It would all be over soon and I wouldn't have to think about it. I wonder if my suicidal peers felt the same way. Were we all so self-involved that we could leave a mess behind without a second thought? Were we all saying one last fuck-you to everyone who cared about us? What if they didn't know why? Would it make it worse? What if they didn't know about the constant pain every fucking minute of every fucking day? I suppose this is why some people leave notes. I didn't care to leave a note. I thought it would make everyone feel worse. "I could've chosen to live with you or die. I chose death. PS, thanks for not noticing." I did feel bad for the people I was going to leave behind, but I'd feel much worse if I stayed.

Vegas on any weekend is a spectacle but Vegas on EDC weekend is magical. It's the regular arresting insanity of Sin City with an additional half a million ravers and partygoers. As I walked in our hotel, the entrance was filled with schools of backpack-toting EDCers, their clothes and luggage plastered with brightly coloured stickers and ribbons. Hotel lobbies were louder than usual and the air was alive with excitement. It was easy to get caught up in it, and I did. There was no reason not to. These were the people I would spend the rest of my life with, and I loved them.

Electric Daisy Carnival was a special kind of rave. More accurately, it's three raves in a row. On all three nights, Friday, Saturday, and Sunday, from dusk until dawn, the Las Vegas Motor Speedway became a heavenly neon circus, if the circus were to include everyone in the crowd as a part of its attractions.

On a normal day the speedway was about a thirty-minute drive from the Strip. With the additional hundred thousand attendees, this drive could take hours. I was still a rookie in this world and hadn't made arrangements for a ride on Friday. I took a cab that took two hours. When I arrived I got through very quickly. After the security gate, I walked towards the racetrack entrance. It was early evening and the sky was getting darker. The warm, breezy June air swept bits of sand onto my skin, a gentle reminder that I was in the desert. I watched in awe as dozens of small groups of costumed friends were jumping, skipping, and dancing their way toward the gates. Giddy with excitement, they adjusted their neon accessories, fishnet stockings, and multicoloured hair.

The Las Vegas Speedway resembled the Roman Coliseum with its soaring curved walls and oversized entranceways. The closer I walked towards the building, the stronger I felt the vibration from inside. I made my way through a narrow corridor leading to the stands. Then I could see it, the biggest rave in the world. I stood overlooking the entire carnival with its fifty-foot stages, multicoloured Ferris wheel, and glowing, flashing costumes in the crowd. It was as if the biggest fireworks show was happening on the ground among the people. Even from afar, the bass pounded my body, every beat leaving me breathless. Music emanated from more than one stage, each piercingly clear, and echoed through the bleachers. I walked down the stands and into the centre where hundreds of people congested the pathways, but nobody cared. On the outside, everyone was there for the same reason, joy. Still, I wondered what lurked behind those cheery painted faces, dilated pupils, and contented grins. Was it a sea of joyful butterflies or were there more people like me looking to escape a reality that was killing them inside?

I passed the foot traffic jam, and was swallowed into the crowd. I made my way to the main stage, Kinetic Field, which hosted the top DJs in the world. It alone held fifty thousand people and never felt packed. If you were to look at the event photos from above, it looked like we stood closely together, but on the ground there was more than enough room to cavort energetically.

I walked over to the bar and bought two double Crown-Bulls (Royal Crown whiskey and Red Bull) and drank them. I bought two more. I walked through the grounds popping pills here and there while visiting each of the six stages. The immensity of Kinetic Field with its fifty-foot stage struck me with awe. I pumped my fist to the various musical subgenres in Cosmic Meadow, but the sultry, alluring thumps of the deep techno stage, Neon Garden, became my personal favourite flavour of Electronic Dance Music.

Walking between stages was just as stimulating. Men in unitards walked along a twenty-foot wall and fell off onto a hidden trampoline that sent them flying back up with no effort. A dozen cyclists tethered by a structure draped in streams of lights resembling an enormous electric snake weaved their way through the crowd. A pirate ship on wheels, with sparkling gyrating dancers waving to the crowd, sailed its way through packs of onlookers, the crew on board tossing out goodies. I'd traveled to an enchanted place surrounded by pixies, fairies, and angels submerged in the depths of Ecstasy and techno music.

Without warning, it became too much. I needed for it to stop, if only for a second. There was nowhere to go and all the lights began to close in on me. Wherever I looked, they were fast approaching. I turned my head away and found refuge in a dark blue plastic Porta Potty. I sat inside, closed my eyes, and took a breath. I calmed myself down, steeped in the fresh aroma of urine and chemical cocktail. I looked at myself in a mirror that was about the size of the palm of my hand. I saw a drunken, greying forty-year-old man who was high on Ecstasy. Dark bags sagged under his glossy, bloodshot eyes. I wondered if everyone outside thought it depressing that some old man was trying to party with them and, sadder, doing so alone. I chanted under my breath, *It will all be over soon.*

It would strike me as weird if I were to witness a man go to a club and dance alone on the dance floor. I don't even think I could do that high, but for some reason it was different here. Maybe it was the open air or perhaps it was the sheer size of the venue. I understood what Jordan meant in *The Great Gatsby* when she said, "I like large parties. They're so intimate. At small parties, there isn't any privacy." At large parties, no one's paying attention. Further, I wasn't able to not dance. Everyone was dancing. I would be the weird one if I weren't dancing. I found my spot and let loose. From a half-stepping head-nod to full on jumping as high as I could, pumping my fist in unison with whoever was around me, I felt a quiet calm in my newfound euphoria. The sweat masked the tears as thoughts echoed in my head: *this is a good place to die.*

I noticed an assortment of flags waving in the crowd. Rave crews came from all over the world and many showed off their country's flag. When I saw a Canadian flag, I made my way over and screamed out, "Ottawa!" followed by high fives and hugs without missing a beat. I made my way deeper into the crowd and towards the stage. The dense air was warmer and the closer I got to the stage the closer I got to other people. In my dizzy state

I stumbled into a couple of guys. I apologized right away. They looked at me still smiling and gave me a high five. "All good!" one said. He saw that I was alone. "Where's your crew?"

"I lost them a while ago," I lied. He made a place for me to dance with them. His muscle-bound friend was quiet and moving sluggishly. He turned to me slowly with heavy eyes.

"It's his first time on X!" said the first guy, laughing. I laughed with him. I noticed that neither of them had their requisite bottle of water, a rule that Chowen had instilled in me. We danced for a while and I saw that muscle-head was still slow. It was much longer than even the first wave of X would last. I leaned in closer to him.

"When's the last time you had water?" I asked him. He shrugged. I fetched us all bottles of water and headed back. I handed muscle-head one and said, "Make sure you keep on these all night. I try to alternate booze and water. It'll get you further into the night...and morning," I joked. He was taken aback and gave me a long hug.

"Thanks man," he said in a slurred voice. I patted his back and we both continued dancing. I don't know why I wanted to help him. Maybe I wanted to do something good before I died. I let the thought pass. I needed to get back to being alone. As soon as they weren't looking, I disappeared into the crowd. It was incredibly easy to lose your friends in a crowd this size. I wandered back to a place in the bouncing masses and took some speed.

I walked to the concession stands to get more alcohol and danced some more. I was lost in the crowd, lost in the world.

The sun began to rise. The night was coming to an end. It had been close to seven hours. My calves were tight from the jumping. My stomach felt like there was something heavy and rotting inside. It was letting me know there would soon be hell to pay. There was no liquid in my eyes and if I tried to shut them, they would only pop back open. When the music stopped, the bass continued to thud in my eardrums. I was swept away in the hordes of exhausted partygoers, and none of us wanted to be seen in the condition we were in. We needed to scatter and hide in dark places.

I found myself in a line for a taxi behind hundreds of people. There was no way I could stay upright much longer. I left the line to find a better way or maybe a place to sleep. I saw school buses taking groups of people back to the Strip. I waved to what looked like one of the drivers. He was a tall man wearing a bright yellow golf shirt and a matching baseball cap. I couldn't make out the logo on either. He waved me over.

"What hotel?" he asked, looking at my eyes which I had trouble keeping on his.

"MGM," I managed to murmur out.

"Okay, it's $60." I reached into my zipped pocket and gave him a handful of cash. I couldn't see clearly or think lucidly enough to figure out what I had given him. He snickered, picked out the money and handed me the change.

The room was still spinning when I woke up. *I shouldn't have drunk so much booze,* I thought. It was five in the evening. Call and text notifications lit up my phone. I saw that Perrine had texted me. She sent me over a hundred texts. They could all be summed up in a couple of messages: "I know who you're with," and "you're disgusting." She could've been talking about almost anyone in my life and I was too tired to try to figure out who. She was hurting and was lashing out. The texts got worse as I continued to read them. "I wish you really did kill yourself." "Next time you try, I'll gladly help." "You are a drug addict piece of shit!" "I'm going to tell your mom you said it was her fault." I didn't respond. I earned her cruelty and it didn't matter. She would get her wish soon.

I was already late for round two of EDC, my final round. Making my way to the bed I texted Chowen, who was only now in Vegas to join me. He told me to get something to eat, drink more water, and meet him in the lobby at seven. I bit a pill of X in half and turned on some music. This would keep me going until rave time. I grabbed the overpriced hotel room bottled water on my bedside table and downed most of it. Eating wasn't on the agenda. I needed the drugs to have the least amount of resistance.

Chowen arranged transportation for us. A local exotic dancer from the Spearmint Rhino, who went by the name Sativa, agreed to drive us. My trinity of drugs—Ecstasy, cocaine, and speed—was securely taped to the base of the shaft of my penis, save a few pills handy for the ride and the lineups to get in. Beside me in the back seat of Sativa's mid-Nineties rusted red Honda was a stuffed green teddy bear, a Care Bear. I sat him on my lap.

"That's Lucky Bear," Sativa said with a wink through her rearview mirror. Lucky Bear looked at me with a big, friendly grin. I'm not sure if he was a superhero but he did sport a dark-blue eye mask and cape. Did he have a secret identity? Maybe he needed time of his own where he would not share his superpower, which apparently was luck. If I saw him on the street, I feel I'd recognize him by the white clovers on his hands. I held onto Lucky Bear for the rest of the drive. We became close friends and I hugged him tightly when thoughts of my life and ending it surfaced. I clearly needed more drugs.

Walking into the venue was less magical than the previous night. The lights were dim without the contrast of a dark night sky. I didn't see the grounds covered in ecstatic, glow-in-the-dark ravers. Instead, an internal battle waged in my body. The hangover and comedown from the previous night fought to take hold while the new drugs attempted to suppress the enemy. Tonight, the new drugs would win. They simply had more firepower.

The three of us made our way to the bar and downed doubles of our go-to drinks. It was time to rally. We popped some pills and started to dance. I was taxiing on the runway preparing for takeoff. If my timing was right, I would overdose for the set of the night, Avicii, on the main stage, which was still hours away. Chowen navigated us from stage to stage to see his favourite DJs. I snuck more Ecstasy and speed whenever I could, but waited to be in one of the Porta Potties to take any cocaine so Chowen wouldn't see. My subterfuge wasn't working very well. Out of the corner of my eye, I noticed Chowen watching me. Too high to be stealthy, I was already clumsy and slurring my words.

"Slow down, man," he said with a concerned look on his face. It was the first time I had seen Chowen with an expression of a chiding adult. Not too long afterwards, he asked me how many pills I had left. This wasn't an uncommon question. Many a degenerated night the two of us would pool and ration what we had to ensure we always had enough, but on this occasion he questioned me for a different reason. Emptying my pockets, I showed him the baggies, leaving the cocaine behind. He didn't know what to make of them.

"There's lots of night to go man. You probably lost track so grab some water and let's chill for a bit." I acquiesced and we headed for one of the many rest areas. We ended up in a place built to resemble gardens from Alice in Wonderland. We strolled through a lush green arch, among teacups larger than we were. We sprawled out together on one of the green leather sofas. I lay there looking at the sky. It was almost time. Chowen broke the silence.

"You okay, man?" Sativa excused herself to go to the washroom, presumably to give us privacy.

"Ya, I'm good. You?" I deflected. The part of my brain in charge of rational thought had left for the evening.

"I'm fine. Did you go too hard last night maybe?" I didn't respond. I couldn't respond. "Maybe chill for a bit and enjoy the rest of the night. We have tomorrow too." But we didn't. There would be no tomorrow. Not if I could help it.

"Yeah, okay." He didn't ask for the drugs I had in my pocket and I didn't offer them to him. I needed them to finish what I started.

"Ready for Main Stage?" he asked, trying to lighten the mood. I gave a thumbs up to avoid calling attention to my slurring. I stumbled when I stood up, and Chowen let out a concerned sigh. I didn't let him help me. I steadied myself and gave him a smile assuring him everything was okay. We walked toward the main stage as the DJ before Avicii continued. The fast-paced, aggressive sound felt like wind pushing us back. We squeezed our way into the middle of the Kinetic Fields crowd ready for Avicii to soon take over. I reached into my pocket and threw a handful of pills into my mouth. I looked at Chowen. He'd seen it. If he couldn't tell what was going on earlier, he knew now. His eyes radiated his sadness, concern, disappointment, rage. I could hear his thoughts. *How could you do this to yourself? How could you do this to me? How could you do this to everyone in your life? How could you?* The baggy holding any remaining pills fell to the ground. I couldn't bend over to pick them up. Chowen stood there looking at me. The winds of the desert outside stirred around me. The music stopped. Sand whipped against my skin. This wasn't the gentle breeze I'd been feeling all night. It was not the drugs. It was real. A sandstorm was hitting EDC as Avicii was about to go on. At the time I was planning to die. A deep, ominous voice echoed over the crowd. "Please calmly walk away from the stage." I fell to my knees. Grabbing my arm and placing it around his neck, Chowen picked me up and walked me toward the stands. I wanted to break free, but I was too weak. Chowen walked my limp body alongside tens of thousands of other frightened rolling ravers. We didn't stop at the stands. Chowen carried me to Sativa's car where I crawled into the back seat. The night was over but I still had my chance. I reached into my pocket to take whatever I had left. There was nothing. I lost it in the crowd. I could only hope that whatever I took would do the job. But I was thankful I wasn't alone. Lucky Bear was still smiling. I clutched him tightly and waited.

We drove the car to one of the exits along with what seemed to be thousands of others. The glowing, magical glitter of EDC became an endless sea of flickering tail lights and interrogating headlights. Our car crawled forward a few feet at a time while Chowen and Sativa smoked their cigarettes and Sativa recited poetry. Music from cars around us drifted through our open windows. Laughing, hollering, and fist pumping from the masses who were not going to let a sandstorm stop them continued in their forced surroundings. We played no music. The car moved its allotted short distance until we had to stop again. The rocking was strangely soothing. I was back to when I was a little boy in the backseat of Joe's car. I wondered where my life had gone. I wondered who I'd become. *Please, let it be over.*

"Fuck, I need to pee!" announced Chowen. Drinking the amount of water that we do when we rave brings with it an uncomfortable side effect. "Fuck," he said again and began looking around. He picked up an empty water bottle from the floor. We could all hear, and smell, the thunderous stream of urine filling the bottle. I also had to go now and tapped his shoulder to make sure he didn't throw out the bottle. He looked at me.

"You have to go too?" I nodded. Chowen waited for the next time we stopped the car to open his door to pour out its contents. Chowen handed me the bottle and I made my way to my knees. The exercise of peeing into a bottle may seem like an easy one, but it's far from it. First, the spout was too small to fit a penis into. I'm not talking about my penis. I'm talking about any penis. It's approximately the circumference of a nickel. This means we have to make sure that the urinary meatus, the peehole, is exactly within this target. If this isn't enough, the head of the penis, the glans, should not be pressed completely against the opening so as to prevent air from coming out as we are depositing the urine. I tried doing this in the back seat of a moving car while overdosing on three narcotics. I couldn't. I missed and peed on my hands, my shorts, and the floor of Sativa's car—although I did somehow manage to get some into the bottle.

As I sat in the back seat holding on to Lucky Bear, it became clear that I was not going to die. I'd failed again. I tried to figure out how much I took. It was something like sixteen pills of Ecstasy, four or five pills of speed, a dozen or so bumps of cocaine, and maybe ten to fifteen double Crown-Bulls. It wasn't enough. I shouldn't have drunk all that water.

It's important to know that although I loved Chowen, I didn't know how much until that night. More importantly, I didn't know how much he loved me or how well he knew me. We hadn't known each other for very long and we only saw each other once every couple of months, during which we'd annihilate ourselves with drugs and alcohol. Maybe he was just an empathic guy, maybe he was getting to know me, or maybe he could simply do the math when he saw how many drugs I'd taken.

I missed the last night of EDC, not moving from my hotel room bed. When I woke up twenty hours later, the emotion of what had happened in the sandstorm overwhelmed me and I cried. I could blame the comedown from the cocktail of drugs leaving my system while my body had used up my serotonin reserve. I could blame Chowen, or the sandstorm itself, for interfering with my intention of dying. These weren't the reasons I was crying. I had failed, again. I was alone again. Certain I'd lost Chowen as a friend, I was about to go home to that cold, empty condo, again. *I hate my life.* I lay there face-to-face with Kevin once more. His eyes looked at me with cocky disappointment as if to say, *You couldn't leave me if you tried.* He was right. He held my hand while I wept some more.

Sativa asked Chowen to bring Lucky Bear to me. "He needs him more than I do," she told him. Chowen surprised me with Lucky Bear when he came to visit me in Ottawa weeks later. My eyes teared when he handed me the bear and told me what Sativa said. She was right. I did need Lucky Bear.

Chowen's post-party poems had become a fun, staple part of our adventures, but the tone changed after EDC. He sent me what he wrote privately a year later.

Mr.
I nearly lost you that night
Until the sandstorm took flight
The lights turned on and the beats shut down,
There were people all around
You told me you didn't care and I told
    you, you're not being fair,
I needed to make you aware of the impact of your stare
A year later I know how much you care
Now you understand how much love is there

Fucking High School

WHEN I MOVED TO MONTREAL UNDER THE CONTEXT OF "problem teen," Dad elected to employ a shock-and-awe approach to parenting. He and Carol made sure I quickly assimilated their established morning and nighttime routines. First thing in the morning, Dad's wife woke up to make coffee. There wasn't a coffee maker with a timer back then. The water was boiled in a kettle. A paper filter folded into a plastic funnel held the coffee grounds, measured out perfectly. The water was poured slowly over the grounds while the pourer watched and waited as it dripped. The coffee was delivered to their bedroom, as my father liked to wake up to the aroma. By this time, my sister and I were woken up to fall in with the morning's activity. Once Dad had a few sips of coffee, he proceeded to shave and shower while his suit was ironed, as he liked the sensation of putting it on while it was still warm. While he was dressing, Carol started breakfast and I'm not talking cereal. Benedict, pancakes, bacon and eggs, or waffles were on the menu. When Dad was ready, he shouted *"Five minutes!"* That meant breakfast was to be ready in five minutes, and my sister and I along with it. We ate together before Dad left for work. Not long after, I'd leave to catch the bus to school. The after-work routine was the same. Dad returned home and went upstairs to change while dinner was prepared. Another *"Five minutes!"* and dinner, along with the rest of the family, was ready at the table.

Ill prepared for this new regime and its dictator, I sunk further inward. Dad imposed his dominance by laying out his rules as soon as I got off the plane. There was no TV from Sunday at 6:00 p.m. until Friday after school. When it was time to pick what I would study at school, Dad selected my courses. Phys-Ed was a waste of time, so that was out. When I got A's in physics, he insisted I transfer to advanced physics, which I failed and consequently was grounded for failing.

When I was sixteen, I was in my room drawing a new type of airplane wing. I'd learned how to make properly scaled schematics in one of my classes, and so I drew up some ideas. I was looking to build a small prototype to see what it would look like in three dimensions. When I asked my father where I could find materials to build the prototype, he laughed and said I was wasting my time since much smarter people than me had already figured it out. I threw my plans into the trash and never looked at them again.

In the throes of boredom at home, I found solace in writing. I wrote ideas for short stories, their characters, and outlined how they would play out. I kept a notebook with me which I labeled "Big Book of Ideas." I wrote whenever I could and if Dad were to check on me, he would assume I was working on my homework. I didn't dare share with him my creative outlet, for fear I would be humiliated once more or, worse, forbidden to continue.

The funny thing about fear running your life is how it is virtually impossible to navigate any type of relationship, let alone the complexities of high school. I was lucky to have Kevin. He knew what to do and that was to hide. Hide from anyone and everyone. Moving from Hamilton to Montreal meant changing education systems. I joined MacDonald High School in the West Island of Montreal in second year, meaning I wasn't already part of any established clique and membership for any of them was not open to new members. I was a skinny, awkward kid with a bad haircut, and was terrorized by bullies almost every day, forcing me to avoid any interaction whenever possible. After a while, I learned where the main terrorists' classes were, and I'd navigate a route to best elude any potential confrontation.

My peers seemed obsessed with material things. They talked about and congratulated anyone who had their own cars. Some sixteen-years-olds already drove brand new Mercedes. They wore the same clothing labels, like Ralph Lauren, Buffalo, Santa Cruz, and Lacoste. Those who didn't clearly couldn't afford it. I was a member of the latter. My Dad, consummately frugal, refused to buy more than what he felt I needed. We went shopping for clothes at Walmart. When I asked for a Sony Walkman, he partially acquiesced, purchasing me the cheapest brand he could find. It was white, not the recognizable yellow, but I was excited to have the escape of music. It broke almost immediately but worked if it were wrapped tightly with black electrical tape. My no-name, zebra-striped music player was able to play my Billy Idol, Phil Collins, and Peter Gabriel tapes. When I discovered hip-hop, it played Public Enemy, Boogie Down Productions, and Big Daddy Kane.

My head was dunked into toilets, the eternal high school cliché. I was beaten on the regular, but one occasion stood out. Carter, a popular tall, blond boy with freckles, along with his clique-mate Blake, flanked me in the school hallway despite my best efforts to avoid them. "Hey, Rob, wanna see something cool?" Blake asked. I didn't respond. "Trust me, you'll like this." I looked down awaiting the fresh torment Blake had planned. "Hold his arm." Carter wasn't sure what was about to happen but he complied and held my elbow against my hip.

"C'mon, guys, I have to get to class." I tried to break free but could barely move. Blake wound up and knuckle-punched my arm right above my bicep. Pain shot through the right side of my body. I screamed a half-muffled yelp and he hit the same spot again and again until I felt a pop. Carter looked at me, surprised. My hand and wrist became numb. When I looked down, the palm of my hand was facing outward. I looked up to Carter's face. It was red with what looked like pity and embarrassment. He let go of me and I slid to the floor holding my shoulder. The two of them walked away, Blake chuckling. The class bell rang and I walked to the nurse's station. The nurse watched me walk in and shook her head. Before I could sit down, she walked over to me to inspect the arm.

"You're going to have to see your doctor. It's dislocated," the nurse said. "What happened?" I told her without naming the assailants. She sighed furiously. "Stay right here," and walked out of the room. The nurse returned with the vice principal.

"Who did this, son?" The VP looked in my eyes intensely. I didn't want to tell for fear of further repercussions from Blake. "We're going to find out eventually and there's no point defending them. We're also going to have to call your parents." *Fuck.* Dad is going to hear about this, I thought. He'll be so embarrassed about me. I bowed my head and didn't say anything. My mind became preoccupied with worry about how this would play out with Dad.

While I sat in the nurse's station, I fidgeted with my arm. I started to pull on my shoulder to see if it would snap back in place. I struggled and flexed and whipped it back until I felt the same pop. I could feel my hand again.

Dad stormed into the school and sternly, stridently, impressively, demanded to see the principal and myself "immediately." I sat beside my father while he yelled at the principal for building an environment that allowed me to get bullied. I watched as my father was the fierce, protective animal he was. For the first time in my life, I felt protected.

The episode only served to reinforce my unpopularity. Not only was I a rat, thus making me a target for more abuse, the principal was now against me too. On the best days, I'd speak to no one. On the worst, I'd end up humiliated and bloody. Years later, when high school students started taking guns into their schools to wipe out the student body, I can honestly say I related to those kids. I understood exactly how they felt. I took up boxing in my twenties and became pretty decent at it. After a few years and a lot of sparring experience, I was at a pub in Montreal when I ran into Carter and other guys that tormented me. It didn't go as I had envisioned, which was one of them saying something condescending or intimidating, followed by me beating them mercilessly. Instead, Carter came over sincerely happy to see me and apologized for how he was back then. I thanked him and shook his hand.

In my last year of high school, I became friends with Russ, a six-foot-four school basketball star who sat beside me in French class, which he hated. Russ carried a handkerchief which he used to blow his nose sometimes during class. The sound interrupted the teacher and everyone had to wait until he was done. I marvelled at his insolence as he shrugged his shoulders as if to say "Hey, a guy's gotta blow his nose." When the class continued, he'd turn to me to show me the heft of snot-load he just blew out and we'd both laugh.

When Russ found out I was being bullied, he made sure everyone knew they'd have to deal with him if it continued. All it took was, "Hey, he's cool. He's with me." Those six words changed my life in high school. Russ also introduced me to Henry David Thoreau when he told me to read Thoreau's essay, *Civil Disobedience*, which led me to his best known work, *Walden*. While my peers dreamed of fancy clothes and cars, I fantasized about vanishing into the woods where I'd build my own home, live off the land, and never have to come in contact with other humans. *Maybe one day.*

Not too long after I met Russ, I met Mark who became another lifelong best friend. Mark was a tall redhead from New York who also played basketball, and the three of us spent a great deal of time together. One of our primary activities, at sixteen years old, was going to parties and drinking alcohol. This didn't reconcile very well with the paternal dictatorship at home, but we managed to squeeze in some drinks at lunch. Russ's and Mark's height got them into our local brasserie, Cousino, so they started taking me. Cousino was a rundown, single room pub that served Molson Export on tap and Labatt 50 in quart bottles. The bartender didn't seem to care as the legal drinking age in Quebec was only eighteen. On most occasions our lunch included frozen egg rolls or grilled cheese sandwiches, both moderately heated in a countertop toaster oven, and washed down with a pitcher of Molson Export. The entire lunch would cost less than ten dollars, with tip. Afternoons consisted of hiding our inebriation from the teachers, a challenge at which we were invariably successful. When teenage drunken afternoons became a mainstay, it was time to raise the stakes.

My father issued an "I'm not your taxi" decree, so I was left to find my own transportation. In the summer, I biked to the closest bus stop, which was forty-five minutes away. In the winter, I had to walk. I didn't want to be at home, so it was my only choice.

An hour had gone by as I walked on a snowy winter day. Quarter-sized snowflakes fell out of the grey sky. My running shoes were soaked through and my toes were numb from the cold. I was halfway to my destination, my friend Donald's house. Donald was a classmate of mine who was also a sort of outcast. I invited myself into his life and I believe he acquiesced out of sympathy. I was passing a row of retail shops that included a Blockbuster Video when I noticed a small red hatchback, a Nissan Micra, with the engine left running. I walked over to it and got in. Still new to driving, my recent driver's education training kicked in reminding me to fasten my safety belt. *Fasten my safety belt? What the fuck? I'm stealing a car.* I didn't have time to fasten my safety belt. I did it anyway and I saw that the car was a manual transmission.

Luckily, I learned to drive on manual cars. I imagined more seasoned car thieves would check for this first. How embarrassing would it be to already be in the driver's seat of the car you were stealing and not know how to drive it? I pressed the clutch and released the brake.

I felt my forehead moisten as I moved the gear into reverse. I turned my head, gave it some gas, and slowly released the clutch. My hands trembling, I shot a look back at the Blockbuster front door. I was still in the clear. I backed into the street and pressed the clutch again. I struggled to get the car into first gear. The stick shift slipped from my hands and I turned to check the store door again. No one. I pumped the clutch and managed to slip it in gear. I gave it too much gas and the car slid into an overturn into the slushy road. I let go of the gas and let the tires take hold of the road just like I learned in driving class. I started to drive. I wasn't breathing and all I could think of was to get away. Evidently, I was so concerned that I didn't notice I was driving on the wrong side of the street. The driver in the oncoming car honked and waved in annoyance as I turned into my own lane, cutting someone else off in the process. I had stolen my first car and it was a rush! I took it to Donald's and showed him what I had done.

"What did you do?" Donald's expression was less impressed than concerned.

"It was in the parking lot running with the keys in it. It was easy." He shrugged his shoulders and shook his head. We took it out for a few joyrides and he advised me the best thing to do was to wipe it down and never use it again. I was disappointed but understood so I drove onto a random street in a foreign neighbourhood and left it there. We went back to school the following Monday as if nothing had happened. I felt like a badass but didn't tell anyone. I had no one to really tell other than Mark and Russ, but they would have berated me and I didn't want to risk losing the few friends I had.

I kept thinking about the car. I wanted the adrenaline rush again. The next Friday, I made my way to where I'd left it in that far-off neighbourhood and was surprised to see it still sitting there. The keys were still on the seat so I decided I'd take it for another spin. I took the car to meet with Donald again where he was visiting with a few of his friends. They lived in an apartment building in Little Burgundy not far from downtown Montreal. The apartment was filled with smoke from the weed they were smoking. When I walked in, the room became quiet and they all looked at me intently. I was the only white person there but it didn't seem to bother them after Donald introduced me. Donald's friends bragged about the money they made dealing drugs. I nodded my head impressed, but I barely understood what they were talking about. I was frightened and exhilarated. They were untouchable. Neal, who seemed to be the leader, laughed hysterically when he found out I had stolen a car. "It's here?" he asked.

"Yeah, it's outside."

"Let's go," he said and headed toward the door. I led him to the little red Nissan and he held out his hand for the keys. I jumped into the passenger side. Neal gave me a cocky, crooked half-smile while he started to drive out of the parking lot. He immediately put the gas to the floor to see how fast we could go.

"I think it just sounds faster instead of actually going fast," I joked. Neal chuckled.

"So whatchu need, man?" I shrugged my shoulders. "I got nine's and six-shooters. Whatchu need?" Neal was asking what kind of gun I'd like to buy. How did I come to be in a car with a guy that thinks that I wanted to buy a gun? I smiled a smile that I hoped made him think that I was cool with what he was asking, but it was more accurately a reflex of being uncomfortable.

"I'm okay, man. I'm chillin'." I was trying to remain as calm as possible, but became curious. "Do you sell silencers?" I was peeking into the rabbit hole. Neal laughed, his eyes still watching the road.

"Nah, that's some movie nonsense." He laughed again. We didn't speak for the rest of the joyride, which didn't last long. When it was over, he parked the car and threw me the keys. "Let me know if you need any, *aight*?" Neal grabbed my hand in cupped handshake.

"I will, man, thanks."

"You coming to the club tonight?"

"Absolutely." Accepting Neal's invitation meant missing curfew and the consequences that would follow. I didn't care. I had new friends now.

I picked up Neal in the stolen Nissan and drove him to the club, which turned out to be a supper club. This meant it was a restaurant that dimmed the lights and played music at a certain time in the night. Since it was really just a restaurant, a sixteen-year-old like me could be inside. The supper club was packed as people congregated to watch a Mike Tyson fight. When the fight was over, which was less than a minute, the music was turned up and we sat at a table where Neal's crew subtly passed me drinks. At some point that night, someone in the crew, possibly Neal himself, bragged about us showing up in a stolen car. Someone, presumably who disliked Neal, called the police who came to check out the tip. The police found the stolen car, Neal, and me. As Neal and I were escorted out in handcuffs, a group of black teenagers with big afros looked on and put their fists in the air. One of them shouted, "Fight the power man! Don't say a word until you talk to your lawyer!" I smiled. I had no idea how to respond but I felt cool. My life had become interesting to someone.

At the police station, an old yellow building with steel bars on small staggered windows, I was fingerprinted and photographed. An aggressive detective with a bushy moustache questioned me. I admitted everything. I was still a minor and they let me know my father was on his way to pick me up. Fuck again. Dad was on his way. What was I going to say? Was I going to get beaten? Was I going to jail? Would Dad let me go to jail? Would he insist I go to jail? Dad didn't say a word to me when we saw me. He looked at me, his expression tired and defeated. He continued his silence the entire, painfully long drive home. I cried as quietly as I could. When we arrived home and walked in the door, he turned to me and sighed. I went to my room. The following day, Dad didn't yell. He didn't tell me how disappointed he was or asked why or how I had done it. I was to go to school, come home, do my homework, have no social interactions, and no television. That was it. My father and I had never been close in my adolescence and this only served to push us further apart.

The next few weeks were more of the same. We were nothing more than blood-related associates. He drove me to the police station to meet the owner of the car who was not only unperturbed, he found the whole thing amusing. He laughed as he told the police he wouldn't press charges, and that it was just a case of boys being boys. Legally, I was let off with a warning.

Now under father-ordered house arrest, I wrote more. My journals became a safe place, a secret best friend. I recorded notes about the characters I created, and where I thought the story could go. I invented friends and punished my enemies. Writing served as a refuge, an alternate universe in which I was surrounded by people who recognized that I was worthy of their respect and their love.

Romantic love continued to elude me until my final year of high school. My first girlfriend, Christina, was a star field-hockey player. Sadly, also a smoker. She was my first sexual experience although at the time I assured her that I had plenty of prior exploits. She realized I was full of shit right away. This was before the internet and porn sites that would have taught me how things worked. In hindsight, had I attempted any techniques learned from those videos I would have probably been punched in the solar plexus.

I fumbled my way through my first time with Christina, either going too fast or too slow. Sex wasn't what I expected. It was a bizarre, slippery enterprise that resulted in ejaculation. That was it. Sex seemed overrated but I felt pressured to do it more.

My perpetual home incarceration did not present many opportunities for social engagements. The only way I could see Christina was late at night when I snuck out of the house, an endeavor not without its challenges. My bedroom sat directly above the living room, which enjoyed large bay windows. Illustrating my dedication to escape I had procured a rope in which I tied multiple knots to use as handles when shimmying down. I biked to Christina's house in the cold Canadian winter listening to an INXS cassette in my imitation Walkman. After a few months of dating Christina, I grew repulsed by kissing a smoker and we broke up. It felt awful to hurt someone, but I didn't want to continue. I retracted back into my shell and spent most of the time on my own until graduation.

Interactions with high school girls continued to be painfully awkward. "Hey Rob, how was the weekend?" asked Kym. It was first thing in the morning and we stood next to our respective lockers. I didn't know Kym very well outside of a simple smile in class or a short exchange about homework. Kym was taller than most of our peers and wore a warm smile.

"Good," I answered nervously, not knowing where to look. My mind began channel surfing. It was as if I was looking for the right thought by examining every single possibility, not unlike looking for the right channel on TV in an endless subscription of choices.

"That's good," she said. "What did you get up to?"

My mind fell deeper into a sea of anxiety. Why was she asking me this? Was she playing a cruel joke? Did she like me? Was she bored? My mouth dried, my heart attempted to punch its way through my chest, and I lost the ability to put together sentences. Kym looked around uncomfortably while she waited for me to answer. I smiled and felt my face warm. Kym nodded and slowly walked away. Kevin was right. I had to avoid any human contact as much as possible. I went to great lengths to dodge any further embarrassments, and kept my eyes down or in my books whenever possible.

In Quebec, college—called CEGEP (say-jep)—was a two-year stint where students worked towards getting into a university or taking another path. College was liberating. No one knew who I was other than the few students with whom I attended high school. Fortunately, it was a big place with many new faces, and although Mark and Russ went to different colleges, the bullying was over. I met some unique people and shared some romances, but none so deep as to merit reflection. Physical connection remained painfully disquieting. Meeting and growing close with someone started to feel natural, but crossing into the territory of sex was fraught with anxiety and trepidation.

Home life was a new challenge. I left my father's compound and was couch surfing as a place to live. My father was, however, financing my academic pursuits. A year and a half of college went by when I decided to move back to Hamilton and live with my mother again. Mom was a recovering alcoholic and deeply immersed in the twelve steps of Alcoholics Anonymous. She wanted out of the lifestyle she had fallen into in British Columbia and moved back. We both needed help.

Criminals and Other Fine Friends

THE FAILED SUICIDE ATTEMPT IN THE SANDSTORM AT Electric Daisy Carnival did not dissuade my resolve to die. Shortly after my return home from Las Vegas, with my body still in the depths of withdrawal, I was invited to party with a drug dealer, Moe, and his friends in Montreal. The idea of being surrounded by violent drug dealers attracted me. My desire to be seen as dangerous persisted in me since I was a teenager, and the reputation I achieved by spending time with Branson only heightened my craving.

We all went to Musique nightclub in downtown Montreal. I was with five other men. We walked past the dozens of people waiting in line and up to the bouncer who unhooked the velvet rope and let us in. The bouncer nodded to me impassively. I nodded back. We walked up a narrow stairway to the inner entrance and were escorted to our bottle service booth. As we walked through the packed club, the distinct rumbling of hip-hop felt like a soundtrack meant just for us. I looked around acting as if I might see someone I knew, while inside I was asking myself why I was here with these guys. I needed to get high fast or panic would set in and I'd have to find a way out of there.

An intimidatingly large, angry looking black man, Gerome, joined us and fist-bumped each of us with hands the size of footballs. I was instantly afraid of him. Moe introduced us and mentioned I was looking to score some Molly and coke. Gerome was the drug dealer's drug dealer. He sold me some Molly and coke and we stayed to drink and party with his friends. I took the Molly immediately and deliberately in front of Gerome. I wanted to assure him that I was not a cop. I was less discreet than I meant to be. Moe grabbed me and told me not to be so obvious. I apologized while Moe subtly snorted a tiny pile of white powder that sat on his thumbnail.

At the end of the night Gerome joined us all for a quick drink at Moe's hotel suite. When I walked in, one of Moe's friends approached me aggressively shoving a small case in my face. It appeared to be some electronics that I didn't recognize. I shrugged and said I didn't know what it was, which agitated him more. He was a big guy but everyone in that crew was muscular and covered in tattoos. All of them had a violent edge to them. They were all drug dealers after all. They spent their time lifting weights and selling and doing drugs. Nothing says fear quite like the realization that you are in a room full of coked-out, muscle-headed drug dealers that suspect you are a cop. Finding the small device in the room did not help. Their paranoia grew. Moe stormed over to me. "I fucking trusted you and you bring this shit here? I fucking vouched for you!" I was dumbfounded. It occurred to me these were the type of people I should be around if I wanted to get myself killed.

"Dude, whatever that is, it isn't mine. It doesn't even look like it's assembled," I said defiantly. When I looked into Moe's eyes, they were barely able to look in one direction. They scanned everything in the room. I decided to leave and walked out. When I walked around the corner in the hallway, there stood Gerome.

"That was pretty fucked up," I said.

He snickered. "They're out of their heads. It happens." We stepped into the elevator together.

"This M is fucking amazing, by the way. So is the coke," I told him. He laughed. He gave me his number and said to give him a shout if I ever needed anything. I now had an out of town drug dealer. I was moving up in the world.

I woke up the next morning strung out. The cocaine combined with the Molly felt like my body wanted to get up and go to the gym while at the same time begging me to slow down and get some more sleep. The sunlight seared through the hotel windows. It was noon and I had to make my way out of the room before I was kicked out.

This would be a recurring theme for my out-of-town drug binges. Hotels were incredibly inconvenient places to recover from being high and partying all night. Of course, I didn't think of this as a red flag about my behaviour, but rather that I had to plan better. When booking I would ask about late check out or simply pay for an extra night. I would accept that the next day I'd be strung out and not know how to be a proper human. I needed to give myself more time to reboot. I saw this as being more responsible.

Gerome and I kept in touch and every other weekend we would connect in either one of our cities. I deliberately made more purchases through him, and I introduced him to friends to increase his client base. I started to invite friends from Ottawa to join me and they seemed to enjoy the darker criminal cachet of the club scene. Gerome was there when Perrine sent vicious texts which pushed me deeper into his scene and, sometimes, into weeklong drug and alcohol binges.

Spending time with Gerome wasn't about a budding new friendship. Nor was it about my continuing to become a full-blown drug addict while attempting to get myself killed or die from an overdose. A new addiction was born. When I was out with him, I was seen with him. I was seen with his friends. I was consorting with known vicious criminals and I liked it. We never waited in any lines at any club. If anyone tried to sneak into our booth or fuck with me in any way, Gerome was the first to physically toss them away. While I liked the high of dancing around and fist pumping like a complete idiot, Gerome and his friends sat around the booth surveying the club as if they were private henchmen. For Gerome, I was the sponsor. I paid the bill for the drugs and alcohol for myself, my friends, his friends, and whatever group of women that happened to work their way into the booth that night. Even the club bouncers and security knew better than to try to enforce any of their arbitrary rules, like no dancing on the sofas, which the girls loved to do in their drunken elation. If one of the bouncers broke rank and tried to enter our booth, Gerome was quick to let them know they were not in charge—sometimes physically.

I went from worrying that I was looking like a drug dealer to reveling in it. And the best part was that I wasn't. If the police investigated me, they would find nothing. I was a drug user, not a drug dealer. Although if they found my stash, it may not look that way.

Gerome had a tight crew and I got to know his friends. Sonny was a kind-eyed, bald French-Canadian. He always wore a smile and gave me and my friends big hugs when he saw us. Nick was a bald, good-looking, muscular Greek who looked you right in the eyes when he spoke to you and tried to find if you were full of shit. Together these men were frightening, exhilarating and attracted a lot of attention, both good and bad.

The good part about being a part of this group was that the club owners were quick to make sure we got the best tables and service, and women attracted to the bad boy life were quick to swoon. The bad part was the group also attracted the attention of the police. Our booths were often raided with "random checks," resulting in each one of us having to provide our identification followed by a line of questioning. What do you do for a living? Where do you live? Who is that and what does he do for a living? I was always overly helpful and cooperative. "I develop software," I'd say. "I'm just a computer geek."

One day Gerome texted me saying he was coming to town and wanted to talk. It was uncommon to have a sober daytime visit, but I agreed. When we sat down, he explained the inner workings of micro loans and how profitable they were. Gerome proposed that we become loan sharks together with me funding it and he collecting the payments. He said he had been collecting for other people for a long time and now wanted to try to do it for himself. We would be partners. This was my chance to tiptoe into the world of organized crime. I asked questions that I thought someone in a gangster movie would ask. Would we have to pay tribute to someone if we were to encroach onto their territory? How bad could it possibly get if someone didn't pay? I didn't want to be in the business of hurting people. I was only in the business of hurting myself. Gerome assured me people always paid. He said his system actually helped and we could even have return customers. This proposal wasn't something I had to think deeply about. I didn't ask Gerome to give me a few days to mull it over so I could consider my options. I wanted in the game. I asked him how much we should start with. He suggested five thousand. I agreed and we were in business.

Every week Gerome updated me about the business over text in code. When we saw each other, he'd bring a cash payment for me which I invariably pissed away on more drugs and expensive bottle service. I wasn't in this business to make money. I was in it for what Gerome and his crew brought, which was what I felt when I walked into a club, the feeling that people were afraid of me, the feeling that I mattered. I was in it for the short few hours when I was treated like I wasn't the insignificant lowlife I believed I was. In those few hours I felt protected from the outside world while, at the same time, I was exposed to being arrested or worse.

Gerome told me we loaned out the entire amount in a few weeks, which meant the payments would start rolling in. And they did. Keeping the loans in a small note-book, Gerome showed me our weekly reports. After a few months of steady payments, I decided to double down on the fund. Gerome made more loans and the payments got bigger. Some of my friends were becoming suspicious as to why I had so much cash around when paying for our nights out. I made up excuses every time. They knew I was lying and I knew they knew I was lying. I wanted them to be suspicious. I wanted them to think there was something going on. I wanted them to think that behind this geeky software entrepreneur was a gangster. And they did.

After the nightclubs, we always ended up at the after-hours clubs where I was reintroduced to GHB, the drug that Michelle and I unknowingly ingested in Las Vegas. This was Gerome's friends' drug of choice. I added small amounts of GHB to my rum and colas. It amplified the feeling of drunkenness, and I had less control over what I was saying and doing. One night I consumed so much, I ended up sitting down on the dance floor and eventually crawled my way to the wall. Nick joined me in my stupor on the ground. No one bothered us. He passed me a small pile of cocaine balanced on the end of a key. "Bump?" I snorted it and thanked him, then started to cry. "Whoa. Are you okay, bro?" I couldn't control it. I wiped my eyes and looked down.

"Fuck...I don't know what's wrong with me." Nick leaned back to do his bump. More tears rolled down my face. I wiped them away as they came. *What the fuck am I doing? I don't want to be here. I don't want to be alive at all. Why can't I just kill myself and get it over with? Am I just too worthless and weak, or am I hoping that I'll get through it? If I'm hoping I'll get through it, then why am I ruining my life by spending my savings and becoming a criminal? I have to end it soon. The money will run out or I'll end up in prison.*

"You good?" Nick interrupted my vacant stare.

"Ya, man. I'm good." I answered. I was no longer crying. "You?" Nick nodded his head.

We sat in silence until Gerome came over and motioned that he was leaving. I made my way to my feet and into a cab outside. The sun blasted my eyes and pierced my brain. The pain numbed with the reminder that I was newly resolute to end my life. *I have to end it. I have to end it as soon as I can.*

Following my crying episode with Nick, the world around me felt further away as if the volume had been turned down and my mind couldn't focus on anything other than suicide. If I secured the necktie on the railing where my feet couldn't touch and I couldn't save myself, it might work. I have enough drugs in my house to kill a small elephant. Maybe I could try overdosing again. Maybe I could do both. I wondered if Gerome could get me a gun. He could definitely get me a gun! That's it. I'm getting a gun to do the job right.

* * *

I had thought about getting a gun before but had no idea how. Did I go to a gun store and fill out an application? There had to be a question about criminal convictions. I was sure, however, Gerome could get one for me. I needed to be discreet so he wouldn't know why I wanted it.

"I have a question for you." I watched the half-filled dance floor. It was still early in the night. "Could you get me a gun?"

"What the fuck you need a gun for?" Gerome looked over to me as he cupped his GHB-laced Vodka Red Bull.

"Just in case," I answered. "I mean, I'm doing stuff

with you now and who knows?" I saw no expression from Gerome.

"I'll see what I can do."

And that was that. I was getting a gun. We didn't speak about it for the rest of the night but the thought persisted. Death was getting closer. The music damped into the background as I lost myself in thought. My death scene projected in my mind. *How will I do it? The shower would cause the least amount of mess and keep Logan safe. Where will I point the gun? Mouth so it can get through the back of my head. I don't want to take the chance of being able to survive.*

A few weeks had gone by when Gerome told me to meet him at my condo at lunch. It was a Wednesday and I made my way home from work to meet him. I assumed it was about the gun but couldn't confirm it over the phone. Anyone could be listening.

"Ssup?" Gerome said as he walked into my condo. He was wearing a navy-blue hoodie and his hands remained in his pockets.

"Yo." Gerome sat at my counter as he always did. He placed a black object on to the countertop. The sound of it hitting the surface sent a spark down my spine but when I looked closer, I saw that it wasn't what I thought it was.

"I didn't get you a gun, but I gotchu this." *What does he mean he couldn't get me a gun? He wouldn't get me a gun was more like it.* Gerome looked over to the small, black belt pager. "It's a taser."

"It looks like a pager from the Nineties." I picked it up to inspect it. I turned the power switch on and touched the button in the center. A clamorous jolt of electricity sparked at the end. *What am I going to do with this? I can't kill myself with this? Am I supposed to be grateful?*

"You don't need a gun, man. You got me and if I'm not around, you have this now."

"Thanks, man. It's cool." I didn't know what else to say. Maybe Gerome knew what I wanted it for. Maybe he was protecting me. My plans to shoot myself were ruined unless I could find another way to get a gun. *Fuck, I need to get high.*

Lifeline

MY INVITATION ACCEPTANCE TO ESCAPADE, ONE OF CAN-
ada's biggest EDM music festivals, came with high-fives
and handshakes from my Ottawa party friends. It seemed
my continual dissipation was impressive, aspirational
even. A sense of pride in my ability to survive these binges
started to emerge. I bragged about how much drugs and
alcohol I imbibed and lived to tell the tale. How long I
went without sleep or food became a badge of honour,
and sometimes a punch line. I continued the depravity
and hatred of my life under the guise of loving it. It kept
people off the scent of my inner turmoil and impending
death. I was also on pace to spend everything I had.

When I arrived at Escapade, I explored the VIP area
and grabbed a drink. I walked to the railing overlooking
the main audience area. The grassy field was slowly filling with young concertgoers sporting ripped jean shorts,
tank tops, and brightly-coloured sunglasses. The area
was much smaller than EDC Las Vegas, and the crowd

wasn't an army of beaming ravers frolicking in the night. It was groups of children, barely legal drinking age, getting sloppily drunk in the hot sun. I turned away to get another drink.

Instead of the safe anonymity of the crowd like EDC Las Vegas, at Escapade, we stood on our own stage with the deliberate intention of being seen rather than being immersed in the music and energy of the people around us. It was befitting as the energy of the people around us in the booth were not the judgment-free, unconditional love of the raving community. It was shallow, competitive, and off-putting. And worse, it messed up my high. Escapade enabled the next phase of my uppity ego of having to be Mister-VIP-best-booth-never-waiting-in-line guy. I also wanted to be surrounded by my criminal friends.

I looked up and saw Gerome walking towards me. He wore his usual angry look, but as he approached I saw a trace of a smile. He gave me a hug. I felt the eyes of my Ottawa friends on us. I introduced Gerome to a few of them and we dove in with drinks and Molly, Gerome with his sips of GHB. He made his way to the back corner of the booth where he perched himself on the back of the sofa ensuring a good vantage point to spot approaching trouble.

In the booth, beautiful young girls made their way to talk to me. They knew I, along with friends, had spent thousands on the table and assumed there was more where that came from. Some grabbed my phone to text themselves from it. They now had my private number. I didn't care. I was swept up in the shallow cachet.

One woman stood apart from the others. She radiated so much energy it seemed she was bouncing. She spoke quickly and pursed her lips tightly when she smiled as if waiting for it to be returned. Her name was Paige. She was unapologetically goofy and had a lightning-fast wit. It was nearly impossible to keep up with her constant puns but I had fun trying. It was as if she were a cartoon whose expression changed after every sentence, while she kept a watchful eye to see if her humour was being appreciated. This was someone I wanted to be around.

Not too long after Escapade, I was invited to another bachelor party in Las Vegas. I was getting tired of the parties, but to say no would mean to stay home alone. I sat on my sofa staring at the staircase that I'd fallen down after fighting my way free from the noose. *Maybe it's time. I can't get a gun and I don't want to wait anymore. I've waited long enough.* I made my way upstairs to my closet where I pulled out the tie. I sat at the edge of my bed holding the tie. Logan, who was sleeping on my pillow, stood up and stretched out his limbs as he looked around with sleepy eyes. He walked over to me and laid his head on my lap. I rubbed him behind the ears and dropped the tie. I curled up on my bed and passed out.

I awoke the next morning confused. I needed another drug-filled distraction from my cowardice and the Las Vegas trip would be it. I wanted my new friend Paige, who seemed like the only person in the world that could make me laugh, to come. In a moment of brazen audacity, I invited Paige and a girlfriend of hers to join me in Vegas. Once assured there would be no expectations beyond friendship, they accepted.

I made many new acquaintances in my party life in Ottawa, but none stood out more than Brayden. Brayden was a fellow tech entrepreneur who sold his startup to a much larger and quickly growing company. His business acumen aside, Brayden was a warm and kind man who extended an infectious smile and wasn't afraid to hug everyone he met. He was going through a breakup of his own and relatively new to the party scene but dove right in. We took turns hosting after-parties at each other's condos, and had long talks about our exes. Some of these conversations were even sober.

When I mentioned that I was going to Vegas, he jumped at the idea. I wanted to impress Brayden when I told him that I was bringing two good looking, fun girlfriends, and he said he would do the same. One of the women Brayden brought along was a gorgeous blonde named Mira. Despite her intimidating allure, Mira was reserved, quiet, and oddly funny. We barely spoke but I found it difficult to not stare at her when she was in the room.

When we arrived in Vegas, I continued in my haste to spend whatever money I had left. Whenever possible I upgraded our bottle service booths and ordered the most expensive champagne. Brayden saw this as the way things were done in Las Vegas and began to do the same. Be it a nightclub or a day club, we acted like we could afford more than we could for those few hours. Although these parties were a part of the descent into the abyss, this trip felt different. These people were not the shallow, indifferent leeches from the club scene. They exhibited genuine interest in each other. They even seemed thrilled to be around me. I found a lifeline in the most unexpected place, Las Vegas.

I made no secret about my love for doing drugs but this new group of friends had no interest and only planned on drinking. I didn't want to do drugs alone, so I persuaded most of them to try Molly with me. By the time the final night rolled around, almost everyone had tried Molly and loved it. My selfishness had altered their life trajectory. They were drug users now.

Paige continued her hyperactive antics the entire weekend, but in a private moment in our hotel room she broke down crying. She had recently found out that her fiancé was cheating on her and feared that she didn't deserve to be loved. We sat on the bed as she wept and recount what happened. I wiped away her tears and held her close. She asked me if she would ever find someone to love her again. I assured her that everything about her was beautiful, and that there was a lineup of good men waiting for the chance to be with someone of her caliber. I was sincere and she knew it. I reminded myself to remain distant. To deliberately keep our relationship in the friend zone. I wanted to keep her in my life for whatever was left of it, and embarking on any kind of relationship, or sex, with her would mean otherwise.

After our final night of partying, after we arrived back at our hotel room in the mid-morning. Somehow, Mira and I ended up alone. We went back to her room and slipped into bed together. After stumbling our way through a few minutes of exhausted, awkward sex, we both passed out. Surprisingly, later that day we all made our flights home. Mira and I said nothing, and told no one about our encounter.

The following Thursday I met up with Paige, Brayden, and Mira at a local Ottawa club where we indulged in a few pills and many drinks. Instinctively, but subtly, Mira and I hovered in each other's personal orbit, unsure if we were welcomed. At the end of the night, Mira grabbed my arm, letting me know she was coming home with me. When we arrived at my condo, we started kissing but something felt off. Although Mira is one of the most beautiful women I've met, I wasn't interested in sex.

"I'm pretty tired." We stopped kissing and I yawned. We made our way to my bed. "So, you're still in school?"

"I am. In the last year in my philosophy degree." We lay on our sides facing each other in the dark. I could hear Logan purring nearby.

"I love philosophy. I took some courses last year. I like

trying to figure out why we do the things we do," I said, trying to impress her.

"That's psychology," she said coyly.

"I mean we as in a collective. The morals and ethics."

"I like the questions that can't be answered: Metaphysics."

"Isn't it unrewarding to never have an answer?"

"Thinking and debating the ideas are the reward. A lot of what happens in our life, we don't find answers to," Mira responded with confidence. I felt closer to her, a feeling more tangible than what Molly tried to fabricate but couldn't, a connection. Our conversation continued but the more we spoke the more we drew closer. Not too long after we made up for the awkward sexual encounter we shared in Las Vegas. We woke up still holding hands.

Paige and I started spending more time together. It occurred to me that Paige's toddler-like antics were exactly what my therapist, Anne, had recommended months earlier. Anne told me to indulge in activities that I may have enjoyed when I was eight. I was still experimenting with this exercise by playing with LEGO and watching *Star Wars* cartoons, but acting silly with Paige was what I missed out on when I was that age. Unbeknownst to her, spending time with Paige was therapy. Although I wasn't interested in her romantically, I loved her tremendously. She was a fellow child and I could be the silly human I needed to be. It was a constant barrage of poop and fart jokes, hyperactivity, and non-stop puns.

Regrettably, we punctuated it with copious amounts of alcohol and drugs.

One night Paige and I were having dinner together at a sushi restaurant in downtown Ottawa's market district. We set aside our childlike jokes to discuss our exes. Without sharing too much, I told her that Perrine was still texting me. I showed her some of the texts. As Paige read the messages on my phone, her eyes filled with sadness and confusion.

Paige looked up at me from the phone. "Rob, you can't let anyone say things like this to you."

"She's hurt. I hurt her."

"That only goes so far. How long has it been?"

"Six months. Shit. Wait. A year?" I was surprised at how much time had gone by.

"She has to move on." Paige handed back my phone. "And so do you." Paige's words penetrated my psyche. I was already planning to move on, but my idea of moving on was suicide. I didn't want to feel the pain I'd been feeling for so long, but something changed at that moment. I'd found a friend that brought me joy without judgment. *Should I reconsider my decision to die? Can I find a way to live without the pain? With a friend like Paige? Could someone like Brayden like me for who I am? Chowen was sticking by me, why not others? I need to tell Paige everything. About the rape, about my decision to die. Maybe if I told her, she could help.*

I looked up at her excitedly. She had inserted straws

up her nose and was clapping like a sea lion while the waitress brought us shots of tequila. *Maybe telling her would ruin what we have. Maybe telling her would hurt her, like I hurt everyone else I cared about.* As quickly as the thoughts emerged to share my dark truths with Paige, and possibly not ending my life, I swallowed them down with shots of tequila. I decided to spend as much time with Paige as I could before I ended my life, but refused to burden her with thoughts of her new friend wanting to die.

Brayden, Paige, Mira, and I became inseparable. Every weekend the four of us found somewhere to be, whether it was in Ottawa, Montreal, Winnipeg, or Las Vegas. If it was Montreal, I invited Gerome and our criminal friends, whose presence served to intimidate anyone around us and keep away the skulking pickup artists in the club. We booked the best booths at New City Gas, one of the world's best nightclubs, then invariably ended up at Underground to pop more pills and dance until late in the morning the next day. We'd gasp in self-loathing as we walked down the narrow staircase to the exit, blinded by the sun's ambush. When we stepped outside it was a normal day for everyone we passed on the street, while our sweat-soaked bodies buzzed and our eardrums and chests missed the pulsating beat of the deep house music. I had spread my disease of drug abuse to them, but at least they seemed happy.

My newfound friendships with Paige and Brayden,

along with a budding relationship with Mira, became more than a distraction from my longing to die. It questioned my decision entirely. But the agonizingly lonely hours of recovery and sobriety continued to serve as a reminder of what real life held in store. Nothing had changed. I continued to be ineffective at work, Perrine's verbal attacks were persistent and cruel, and I was quickly running out of money.

* * *

One Friday night, Brayden and I went to dinner with, uncharacteristically, no party plans. Brayden mentioned that an EDM Trance rave, which had been famous in Europe, was taking place that night in Toronto. A smile lit up Brayden's face when I nonchalantly suggested we go. Toronto is a five-hour drive but only a fifty-minute flight. There was also a flight every hour. It was eight in the evening when we decided that we were going to take on the challenge of getting us into the event before midnight. There was a second challenge. According to the website, the event was sold out. We didn't let these minor details deter us. We jumped into the car and headed to my place to grab whatever I needed to spend the night in Toronto.

Brayden and I made an atypical agreement. We agreed that this was not to be a bottle-service or VIP night. This was somewhat of a sacrifice for Brayden, as we saw there was a VIP package available that included backstage passes to meet the DJs. Brayden was a connoisseur of trance DJs, and would have loved to meet some of these performers. Still, he opted to hang out with me instead. Here was someone that was kind beyond measure, intelligent in both business and engineering, and he chose to spend time with me. I couldn't grasp why. He had his own money so wasn't interested in mine, and he was with Paige, so he wasn't looking to prowl for women. It was just two friends out enjoying music together. I tried not to overthink it.

As we bounced our heads to the music, Brayden explained who was who and identified the type of sub-genre that was playing. I could barely hear what he was saying, but nodded anyway. The place started to fill up, and we danced alongside hundreds of other ravers, many of them donning bright neon clothing, glow-in-the-dark lipstick, and face paint. Transfixed by a necklace made up of glow sticks, I approached the guy who was wearing it. A thick long dark beard cupped his youthful eyes. As he danced, I tapped him on the shoulder. He turned to me without breaking stride and continued to bounce as he lowered his head to hear me.

"Are those for sale somewhere?" I pointed to the necklace. He shook his head. "Can I buy that one from you?" I thought it couldn't hurt to ask and it was how things were done in Vegas. In my misguided, egocentric mind, I thought he'd want to make some money. He stopped dancing and walked closer to me.

"You can't *buy* light," he said, smiling. He took off his necklace and put it around my neck. I held my new jewelry, dumbfounded, and thanked him. He gave me a hug. I looked up to see Brayden talking to another raver who seemed to be in my new friend's group. I watched as the raver's face lit up, evidently from something Brayden had told him.

"Really?" he yelled. Brayden laughed and nodded his head. "Wow!" The raver walked over to recount what Brayden had just told him, which was how we only learned about the event a few short hours earlier and flew in to attend. They looked at Brayden and me in awe, then introduced themselves. Isaac was the generous soul who gifted me his necklace. Jackson was who Brayden started the conversation with, and Eran was the last of their trio who punctuated his speech with a stoner-like chuckle. Jackson was a tall, well-built man in his twenties. He was shirtless which wasn't uncommon at a rave, and I would have been too if I had a physique like his. Eran was a thin, wiry guy who danced like a marionette whose puppeteer was wildly flailing his handles. It was shocking and hilarious when he was in his groove.

The five of us danced into the early hours of the morning. When Jackson learned I was still new to the rave scene, he sat me down on the dance floor and handed me a pair of refraction glasses that made the world look like a kaleidoscope. Then he had a friend perform a hand light show for me. The friend wore gloves fitted with tiny lights at the fingertips, and moved his hands and fingers in a choreographed dance. It was a sensory overload when high on a substance that amplified your senses. I became unsteady and quickly realized why Jackson had me sit on the floor.

Jackson, Isaac and Eran, or the "Torontos," as Brayden and I began to refer to them, were deeply experienced in the rave scene—a scene which I only then realized I knew very little about. I was a tourist who enjoyed the camaraderie and music, but didn't delve into the raver philosophy. I didn't even know there was a raver philosophy.

"Do you go to raves a lot?" asked Jackson. We had just ordered a round of drinks at the bar during a much-needed break from the dance floor.

"I go out a lot but there's not a lot of raves in Ottawa," I admitted. "Oh, but I did go to EDC this year." Jackson's eyes opened wide. EDC is the Mecca of the rave community. He held his hand up in the universal peace sign and pointed it towards me. Confused, I found it oddly funny and smiled.

"You don't know PLUR?"

Now Jackson was confused. Anyone who attended EDC would surely know what PLUR was. Embarrassed, I told him I did not.

"Wow, you really are new to the scene," Jackson said, laughing. "Peace." Jackson held up the peace sign again and grabbed my hand to do the same. Our two upright fingers touched. It was a secret handshake. "Love." He curled in his fingers and thumb into a curve. I made the same configuration. With our fingertips and thumbs touching, our hands formed a heart. Enthralled, I felt my lips form a huge smile. Jackson continued, "Unity." We interlocked our fingers above the back of each other's hands. "Respect," he finished by sliding one of his beaded bracelets over to my wrist.

"But I don't have one to give back," I said.

"It doesn't matter. Sometimes you do, sometimes you don't." He let go of my hand. I looked down at my new gift. PLUR. Peace, Love, Unity, Respect. The Raver Philosophy. It's how they treated each other. It was how they wanted to be treated. It was a current-day hippie movement.

"Thank you, Jackson," I said seriously. I was grateful not only for the bracelet, but for all the kindness. The "Torontos" continued to educate me in the Ways of the Raver. To protect their hearing, they wore special earplugs that turned the volume of the event down without muffling the sound quality. They wore dozens of bracelets called Kandi on their arms. Some to keep, some to give away. They had backpacks made to carry water, leaving no reason to hold and waste water bottles, and they brought mini-iPods to listen to while leaving the venue to soften the music's abrupt stop.

Brayden and I enjoyed our new friends so much we decided to stay in the city to join them in another night of partying at Toronto's biggest EDM venue, Guvernment. Falling back to my ego, I arranged for the club to have a special booth ready for us in order to thank our new friends for their kindness. Paige joined us in the festivities. Jackson, Isaac and Eran brought along their girlfriends as well. We drank, popped Molly, and danced until most of the partygoers had left. As our group continued to dance in the middle of the now near-empty dance floor, Paige turned to Jackson. "You know those sketchy, tweaked-out people that you see at the end of the night?"

"Yeah, that's us," Jackson assured her. We all laughed but knew it was true. In our self-imposed vertigo, we were sketchy, "tweaked out." We acted like we didn't care. But I cared, and I'm sure each one of them cared too. Call it the Club Scene, the Rave Scene, Drug Scene, PLUR, hippies movements—we were all lost. We were all looking for something that we didn't have. It would be romantic to say that we discovered what we were missing in each other, but we didn't. We found our refuge in drug-fuelled, music-infused nights. We found it in the anticipation of the next high and in the reliving of past events. It was all a perfect delusion of what we were avoiding. A sober look at ourselves. The few hours we were together, we would be okay; each night a warm, manufactured solace from the misery of our daily lives. Each night melting away a small piece of us like a lost glacier in a warm sea.

"Adult"

AFTER MY STINT AT CEGEP (COLLEGE) IN MONTREAL, I
moved back to Hamilton. I was eighteen years old and
moving back in with my mother in another shitty apartment. Moving back to Ontario meant that there was
no CEGEP, and if I wanted to get into university I had
to go back to high school for grade thirteen, a setback
I embraced. I wasn't any older than the other students
but it still felt like my life was moving backward.

I found work at local restaurants mostly in the kitchen
as a dishwasher or prep cook. I didn't get tips and I went
home steeped in the smell of the day's food. If I were in
the "dish pit," I could wear my earphones and keep to
myself for hours. At times, I used my hands to scrape
off the half-eaten food from the plates piled up beside
me. Although it was faster this way, food collected in my
fingernails. The jobs were minimum wage but the people
I worked with were laid back. Many of them commented

on my work ethic and all of them were surprised when I was arrested.

I met Jodie in math class. She had a habit of hiding her smile behind her hair. That made her seem shy, but if she glanced up at me it looked more like she was flirting. She smiled a lot when we studied together and it didn't take long for us to start dating. We spent a lot of time in her apartment where she lived with her mother. When Jodie tried to introduce me, her mother slurred her words and appeared unable to get up from her sofa. Her friend, an older bald man who sat beside her, didn't even look my way. When we escaped to her bedroom, Jodie confided he continually brought her mother booze keeping her drunk every day and that he was married. When Jodie tried to discuss it with her mother, fights would ensue with no resolution.

At this time of my life, I wanted to be a gangster—possibly from the movies, possibly from my perpetual fear, definitely in the absence of any moral compass. Because of my brush with the law after stealing the car in Montreal and the high I felt when Neal's crew of violent thugs respected me, I believed if people saw me as a gangster I'd no longer be afraid. I saw the cheating alcoholic husband as an opportunity to both stop him from bringing Jodie's mom booze and possibly make some money at the same time.

It was a sticky hot summer day. In my mother's apartment, I sat sweating in my bedroom both from the heat and the tensions about what I was about to do. After finding out the name of Jodie's mom's married friend, I found his home phone number in the white pages of the phone book. I picked up the phone and dialed his number. "Hello," a man's old, gravelly voice answered. My entire body jolted as if I'd licked a battery. I inhaled forcefully.

"May I speak with James, please?"

"Speaking." I scrambled for words. It was too easy to find him and get him on the phone. I hadn't rehearsed what I was going to say.

"Uh, hi. I have some information I think you might be interested..." I stammered. "Actually, you don't know me, but I know you."

"Who is this?" the voice asked sternly. This was before the days of call-display.

"Doesn't matter. I know you're cheating on your wife and I don't think you want her to know about it." I began to feel justified in what I was doing. He was the one cheating on his wife. He deserved to be punished and if I could get him to stop it, might help Jodie's mom recover. I was the good guy. There was silence on the other end. "You still there?"

"What do you want?"

"I want you to stop seeing your mistress and I want fifty thousand dollars cash." I was no longer the good guy. I have no idea where fifty thousand dollars came from. More silence. I waited.

"Okay," he said. *Okay?* My heart raced and I punched

the air in celebration. I got him. "How do you want the money?" I had seen enough television to give me an idea on how to get money without being caught.

"Friday morning, I want you to put the money in your trunk, then park your car in the parking lot outside of O'tooles Pub on King Street. Leave the key to your trunk on the rear passenger side tire. Then walk away." I waited for his response.

"Okay, I can do that," he said. The deal was done.

I planned the money pick up with a friend who shared my desire for the mob life. We decided to sleep in my friend's car in front of James's house the night before to see if there would be any police with him. The next morning, we watched as he left his house alone. We followed him to O'tooles, parking behind the restaurant's strip mall. We saw James walk to his back tire to leave the key before walking away. We climbed to the roof where we scanned the area for any police who might be watching. The sun felt heavy on our backs as we surveyed the parking lot. We walked to his car slowly. I made my way to the passenger side rear tire still not looking directly at the vehicle. I pretended to tie my shoe and knelt to see if the key was there. It was. I reached for it, stood up, and put the key in my pocket. I looked around some more and gradually stepped toward the trunk. When I got to the trunk, I inserted the key and turned it. The trunk popped open. Inside I saw a large brown leather bag. My body froze when I heard tires screeching all around me.

I didn't look up when I heard shouting voices telling me not to move.

When I finally lifted my head, I saw loaded guns pointed at my head. I was told to put my hands on the car, but my body turned to stone. I looked up to see my friend's head slammed into the side of the car. Mine followed face first. My lip swelled up immediately. They took me to a police station where I sat alone in an interrogation room for what seemed like hours. Finally, a man with a thick dark moustache stormed into the room. He wore a dress shirt with the top three buttons undone as if he had seen too many Seventies cop movies. He looked at me with eyes filled with repulsion.

"You know what I call blackmail?" he barked at me. "I call it being a pussy. You're a fucking pussy." I'd seen enough *Law and Order* TV shows to know not to say anything, but this guy scared me. I didn't respond, which he treated as an act of defiance, but I simply had no answer. "You're not so tough now you're not on the end of a fucking phone, right pussy?" The detective threw an empty chair against the wall. It bounced and slid back towards him. My gaze left the table just long enough to watch the chair fly. He didn't take his eyes off me. Paralyzing fear washed over me as I realized that I was alone with this man who could hurt or even kill me. Should I just confess to everything so that he would go away? My mind flashed back to high school where I would do anything to avoid a potential confrontation and subsequent beating. Kevin started shouting now too, and told me to tell him whatever he wanted to know.

"Are you fucking hearing me, asshole?" snapped the cop. Kevin disappeared and something, deep inside me surfaced. He couldn't kill me. He couldn't even hurt me. It's why he threw the chair instead of hitting me. He was just trying to intimidate me so he could get a confession. I was just a number to him. *Fuck this guy*. My shoulders relaxed, my heart slowed, I caught my breath. I looked up from the table and into his eyes and unhurriedly, unyieldingly, smiled. *If you want to kill me, kill me, but I won't be afraid anymore. I'm not going back to being that high school kid.* The detective walked out. It didn't matter that I didn't confess. They had more than enough evidence to convict me. But for that short second, I was victorious.

Another hour went by, then another detective told me that I could make a phone call. He escorted me through an open area where I could hear a group of cops laughing. They were talking about how impressive it was that a seventy-seven-year-old man, James, was still able to get it up to cheat on his wife. Their voices hushed as I walked by. I found a criminal lawyer in the Yellow Pages and I made a collect call. My lawyer asked if I had said anything and I told him that I didn't. "Good, keep it that way. Someone from my office will be there shortly."

I sat in a holding cell which was so cold I could see my breath. There was a steel toilet and a body-sized shelf meant to be used as a bed. A man in an adjacent cell asked for food, addressing the officer as "boss." After I was safely locked away, the officer tossed a peanut butter and jam sandwich sealed in plastic wrap into each of our cells. The police took my shoelaces and belt to prevent me from killing myself, but it didn't stop me from trying. I attempted to hold my breath hoping I'd pass out. It only made me dizzy. The realization that I would have to tell my mother what I'd done washed over me. It would break her heart, which would break mine. Maybe I should've thought of that before trying to be a gangster.

When my lawyer showed up, we met in person in the interrogation room with the flying chair. He told me that he'd contacted my mother already to ask her to attend my hearing. I struggled to not break down in front of him. Paying attention to what he was saying, a task I desperately needed to do, was just enough distraction for me to keep it together. Unfortunately for me, it was a Friday and my hearing wouldn't be until Monday, so I was transferred to the Hamilton-Wentworth Detention Centre for the weekend.

The shackles I wore echoed as I walked to the white van where another inmate sat across from me expressionless. We walked into the detention centre through a guarded back door that seemed ten inches thick, and made our way to a room painted yellow and cut in two by a steel fence with a door. Before we could walk through the door, a muscle-bound security guard holding a baton stopped us and barked out orders.

"Time to strip, boys." My van mate started undressing. I did the same while the guard watched impatiently. Each of us stood nude in the middle of the room for inspection. The guard peered into our mouths, nostrils, then had us bend over and spread our cheeks. My mind left the room. *What's going to happen to me in here? Am I going to get raped? Stabbed? Where the fuck is Kevin?*

Six of us stood in a row in the hallway just outside the common area. The guard, a muscle-bound man with a military haircut, looked at his clipboard. He shouted my name in a gruff drill sergeant's voice and I raised my hand. He looked down at me. "These are some big charges for a little guy." I shrugged. What could I say? The guard was annoyed at my lack of response and asked, "Pardon me?" He moved his face close to mine. His frustrated breath drifted into my face like a dragon ready to blow fire.

"Um, yes sir," I managed to squeak out quickly. He moved on dismissively.

I shared a room with a mousy quiet man who kept looking down at his hands while he picked his fingernails. He barely nodded when I entered. Since he was already in the bottom bunk, I took the top. During the day, the doors to the rooms were open to the common area and we could walk to the washrooms and kitchen at will. I was given a toothbrush that was cut in half and a spoon to eat with, which I had to return after using.

The common room was small for the dozens of inmates, and it became smaller every time I glanced around. If I looked around too much, claustrophobia gripped my chest, making breathing difficult. Nothing, not even Kevin, could change the fact I was trapped in a room with convicts. Convicts like me I suppose, but not really. I was miles away from being a hardened criminal and I no longer wanted to be one. Thoughts flashed by in a flickering panic. *How can I get out of here? I couldn't even if I tried and if I tried, I'd be in worse trouble, and if I tried and succeeded it'd be even worse. What if I get raped? What if I get stabbed and no one found me until it was too late? Why did I break Mom's heart? She must be home crying. I'm so sorry. It was that fucker James's fault. No, it's not. It's my fault. I didn't have to try to extort him. I shouldn't have asked for the money. I'm not cut out for this. If I make it, I'll be better. If I make it.*

I caught my breath and calmed down. I watched a few people play cards, work out, play board games, and watch TV. I didn't speak to anyone nor did anyone speak with me. When Monday morning came, I was taken to a room in the courthouse to meet with my lawyer. "We have a deal on the table from the crown prosecutor. It wasn't easy to get. If you plead guilty to a charge of intimidation, you may get off with community service or possibly a maximum of two years less a day, but out in six months with good behavior. It will depend on the judge, but I think we have a good chance of getting the community service. If you try to plead not guilty and we lose at trial, you could be facing up to ten years. It's up to you." The lawyer spoke quickly but I didn't spend much time thinking about it. I was guilty and I needed to admit to it.

"Let's take the deal," I answered. "And thank you."

I entered the courtroom where I saw Mom waiting in the pews. Sadness washed over me when I realized she had just witnessed her son walking in shackles.

The judge accepted my guilty plea and allowed for me to leave on bail until sentencing. When I saw my mother in the hallway after I was released, neither of us spoke. She just hugged me and we went home.

The idea of going back to jail terrified me, as my lawyer's voice echoed in my mind, "two years less a day." There was no way I was going back. I'd kill myself if I had to go back. I started to believe that going back was unavoidable and I acted as if I no longer cared about my life. The epiphany about being better than the criminals I saw in jail was short lived. I began to act out even more. Mom and I screamed at each other daily. She was losing patience and threatened to have me put back in jail until the trial, so I did the only thing that made sense to me: I ran away.

I slept under a fallen tree in a wooded area not too far from where we lived. After having brushed away the branches and dead leaves that lay beneath the tree, I slid in layers of folded cardboard boxes. The local grocery store had plenty of them free to take away. I fashioned a makeshift roof with some more cardboard for the first night, but knew the rain would do away with it quickly if I left it too long. I was finally Henry David Thoreau. My high school fantasy had materialized. Each morning when I woke up, I went to a friend's house where he fed me, then we'd play basketball or I'd go back to the woods. A few days went by and my friend told me that my mother was frantic, but I was too afraid of going home and even more afraid of going back to jail. Mom didn't call the police. She just wanted to know I was safe. After a particularly cold and rainy night in the woods, I called Mom from a friend's house. She agreed to see me and then to let me come home. When I returned, we hugged and wept. She gave me some ground rules like a curfew and some chores. I followed them without complaint.

In the weeks that followed, I'd received notice that I'd been accepted to attend Carleton University in Ottawa. I'd forgotten I even applied. I didn't know if I'd be in jail when the time came to go, but my mother was overjoyed at the glimmer of hope. When I told my lawyer, he said this would help us with sentencing which was scheduled for two weeks before I was to begin at Carleton.

On the morning of the sentencing, I was exhausted. I hadn't slept. I was still terrified of being sent back to jail even for a short time, so I came up with a plan. I found a shaving blade and taped it to the inside of my forearm. If I were sentenced to go back to prison, I'd be taken away on the spot. If that happened, the moment I was alone I'd slash my wrist. I was ready. I dressed up in a borrowed brown suit two sizes too large and we went to the courthouse. Mom and I sat in the pews as we waited for my name to be called.

"Imbeault, Robert," a burly bailiff called to the room. I looked around and my lawyer motioned to me to join him as we made our way to the bench.

"I see you've made a deal with the crown," said the judge as he read my file. He set a folder down and looked at me intensely. "Do you plead guilty to the charge of intimidation?"

"Yes sir," I said. My voice and hands trembled. He watched me closely. My lawyer spoke up to point out that this had been my first offence, that my mother was here to support me, and that I'd recently been accepted to university. The judge listened without looking away from me. I didn't know where to look. If I looked him in the eyes, it felt I was taunting him. If I looked away, I felt I was disrespecting him. I looked down in shame and confusion while he contemplated my fate.

"This is your one chance. If you mess it up, you'll go to jail for a long time. Your life will never be the same. Do you understand me, son?" His voice rose in volume with every word he spoke.

"Yes, sir." I looked him in the eyes. He exhaled a windy sigh.

"One year probation and one hundred hours of community service." The gavel echoed throughout the courtroom. My shoulders dropped in relief. I heard Mom's muffled cry from the pews.

"Thank you, sir," I offered. The judge looked at me expressionless. The bailiff announced another name.

Although I was relieved that I'd avoided going back to jail, I still had to go on living. Living in a world I still hated. I was now even more pathetic, having tried to be something I wasn't. I wasn't a gangster; I was barely able to make it through two days in jail. All I could do was move forward. Take baby steps with the sliver of hope in a new city, and maybe an education. With my university acceptance, I was able to transfer my probation and community service to Ottawa where I'd be attending Carleton University. I hugged my mother at the bus station and headed for the nation's capital.

* * *

It was still summer when I arrived in Ottawa a week before my first class. When I walked through downtown in the thick heat, it felt as though I was a visitor from a faraway land. I strolled through the sea of tourists admiring the Canadian parliament buildings that sat yards away from a cliff overlooking the Ottawa River and into Quebec. The gardens and statues stood immaculate as I made my way to the ByWard Market, which hosts blocks upon blocks of restaurants and bars. Patios, built only for the summer months, were filled with drinking, laughing masses while cars slowly rolled by navigating around the foot traffic. The air felt cleaner, fresher than Hamilton or Montreal. The people returned smiles when you passed them on the street, even when it was busy. When you walked towards a doorway, the person ahead of you looked back to make sure the door wouldn't shut on the next entrant, sometimes holding it open with a smile. It seemed that Montrealers never regarded the next person, while Hamiltonians were more likely to slam the door deliberately. Ottawa felt kinder, quieter.

When I arrived in Ottawa, I received help from my Uncle Garry and Aunt Lucille. They not only organized a place for me to live, they generously let me use an old car of theirs, a 1985 Chevrolet Cavalier. Uncle Garry, a retired air force officer, believed all I needed was a little help and encouragement to get me on the right track. "I have no doubt you are going to be someone great!" He handed me the keys to the car. When I looked up to thank him, his gaze pierced my eyes with a depth of sincerity I never experienced before. I stood still, savouring the immeasurable droplet of encouragement I so desperately craved. I clung to his words, as if they were a bag of priceless jewels. They solidified in my body and for months inspired me to get to my classes and my new job on time.

I did marginally well during my year at Carleton, but not well enough to stay. Unfortunately, I had nowhere to stay in Ottawa and hadn't made many friends, so I returned to Hamilton where I slept on a friend's sofa in his one-bedroom apartment. I found a job in a kitchen as a line cook while I saved money to get my own place. I was back where I started, with nothing.

The friend I was living with suggested we go out to a bar and get drunk to help cheer me up. Reluctantly, I agreed. A few drinks in, I noticed a woman looking at me from the dance floor. She walked over and boldly introduced herself. Her name was Gianna. We spent the rest of the night drinking and telling bad puns. She gave me her number and not too long after we began dating. A few months later we moved in together in Ottawa.

The apartment Gianna found was a small one-bedroom apartment in the west end of the city. The building, poorly named The Phoenix, resembled the roach motels I'd lived in my youth in both aroma and insect life. The first night I spent with her in the Phoenix, we were awakened by a gunshot blast in the hallway. It didn't help the internal constant fear I felt, but I was too proud to admit my anxiety to Gianna.

In our first days and weeks, Gianna and I devoured each other sexually which was followed by holding each other's hands as we fell asleep. Over time, however, what seemed like a loving, safe place became another potential place to get hurt.

"What will you do when she leaves you?" Kevin was always there for me. Protecting me from inevitable heartbreak. "You should probably step back and not commit to protect yourself." I felt this was solid advice. I didn't need more pain in my life and so I pulled away from Gianna.

For weeks at a time I wouldn't speak. I went to work at coffee shops or retail stores while she attended school, and when we went to bed we'd have sex and fall asleep with few words. When Gianna asked about my silence, I'd tell her I was tired. At night after she fell asleep, I broke down. I woke Gianna often.

"What's wrong?" Gianna moved closer to rest her head on my chest.

"I don't know." This was my honest answer on most nights. It was beyond my control. Other nights, I wouldn't respond at all.

"One day you're going to have to tell me what this is about," her soft voice, full of concern and patience, whispered one night. I never did.

"Maybe you should see somebody," Gianna slid in without looking at me as we watched a movie one night. The movie was *12 Monkeys* and was set in a decaying mental institution. The implication was clear. Gianna thought I was going insane.

"Why? So, I can sit there and whine? It isn't going to change anything." Gianna's expression revealed a subtle wave of disappointment. She said nothing. I dismissed the idea quickly but it resonated, then festered. Thoughts started to attack me while I sat there defenseless. Am I starting to lose it? Do I need to be medicated? Committed? Will I end up in a mental institution?

"I think it's where we're going to end up, buddy," Kevin spoke up. "It's the only place we can be truly safe."

Shit, two against one. It was as if my body were being electrically shocked with low voltage. It wasn't enough to knock me out, but strong enough to prevent my limbs from moving. I didn't want to end up in a mental institution. If I ever went, I'd be stuck forever in a daze of drug-induced shackles unable to make any of my own decisions. I could get lobotomized and lay in a broken wheelchair drooling in front of a television for the rest of my life. I turned to Gianna.

"Please don't ever let anyone put me in a mental institution!" I begged. She smiled and looked at me assuming I was joking. "Promise me." When she saw the anxiety in my expression, her smile disappeared.

"Of course not," she said, rubbing the back of my shoulder, "I promise." Ironically, it occurred to me shortly afterward that this request alone might suggest that I should be committed, but I trusted Gianna's word. Kevin tried to bring it up often, and every time I'd shush him and insist that Gianna restate her promise. She did every time, and she didn't pursue the topic further.

* * *

When the school year was over, Gianna and I went back to Hamilton so she could spend time with her family during the summer months. I followed her and rented a room in the basement of a rooming house. One of the highlights of that summer was that it was the World Cup, and Italy was in the finals with Brazil. Gianna's parents, siblings, aunts, uncles, cousins, and friends all crowded around Gianna's parents' television to watch the final game. After an intense match, and no score for either team, Brazil led by one goal in a round of penalty kicks. In Italy's one last chance, Roberto Baggio, dubbed the "Saviour of Italy," flubbed his penalty kick over the crossbar. Brazil won. Hamilton had a large Italian population, so it wasn't a surprise to see dozens of cars honking and cheering on their team throughout the night, even in defeat. Gianna and I decided to join the convoy and waved the Italian flag out the car window. Gianna's sister and two teenage cousins came along for the ride. When the parade subsided, we drove to a local Hamilton hang out spot known as The Beach.

The Beach resembled a scene out of a 1950s movie. It had a diner famous for its fish and chips, and massive amounts of parking alongside Lake Ontario. It also had its own unsavoury elements. While we were driving there, the girls were still waving their flags when the car next to us started shouting obscenities at us. They weren't Brazilian or Italian or even soccer fans. It seemed they were annoyed at all the flags being waved in the streets. One of them on the passenger side was incredibly aggressive. I responded in kind, not really making note that there were four men in the car and it was just myself with three young girls.

We stopped at a traffic light around the corner from

The Beach. With a car in front of us we were now blocked in with medians on both sides, and their vehicle behind us. They jumped out of their car and came to the passenger side where I was sitting. Mistakenly, I rolled down the window to see what he wanted. The first chubby guy started hitting me through the window. I tried to hit him back, but my seat belt tightened and I had to take a few shots to the side of my skull while I unbuckled it. I was able to get out and rushed the one hitting me. I managed to connect with some wild punches of my own, but quickly ended up on my back. By this time, all I could see were boots coming at me. Through the corner of my eye, I could see a crowd forming but no one helped. I felt a hard kick land in my face that left a front tooth bent in to the roof of my mouth. They dragged me over the concrete and I saw one of the other guys deliver a devastating body blow to Gianna. She went down hard. Someone screamed that they had called the police, and the men spat on me and left us on the side of the road. I crawled over to Gianna as her sister and cousin were holding her and crying. I had failed to protect her. I'd failed being a man. I lay there trying to hold Gianna but passed out.

I remember sitting on a gurney while being questioned by a police constable in the hospital. I remember leaning forward on my bed as the sheets stuck to my back, blood from being dragged on the concrete. I remember tonguing my tooth the whole time and pushing it back to its original position with my fingers, trying to hold it in place. The constable told me to get the tooth looked at as soon as I could because if I didn't, it would surely turn black and rot. I didn't get it looked at since I couldn't afford the luxury of dental work. It hurt like hell every day for months, but it didn't turn black or rot.

As the memory of the attack faded so too did my urge to retaliate. I was set to move back to Ottawa shortly and any time the topic was raised, I was encouraged to stay away, to let it go. The result of the Hamilton beating, and the many I received in high school, served to intensify my paranoia. Kevin was never too shy to remind me. I was beginning to think he was right about the psych ward.

The Streak

"EAT, RAVE, SLEEP, REPEAT." READ A FRIEND'S T-SHIRT. OUR new motto. It occurred to me that this motto must be popular given that the T-shirt existed. I wondered how many other lost souls like me were among them. My tribe within a tribe. I wondered how long they had left.

Unexpectedly, another year escaped me. Nonstop drug use has a way of subtly stealing away time. Mira moved in with me. It was convenient for her as she was finishing her degree at Ottawa University which was near my condo. Mira's studies seemed to come easy to her. Even with our full-time party schedule, she managed high grades and consistently delivered her work on time, albeit every so often very close to the deadline. Mira was also working at a restaurant part-time, but her shifts interfered with our party nights. Not too long after she moved in, I encouraged her to quit.

Our sober nights, when not consumed by recuperation from the night before, were loving, respectful, fun even. We brought up the idea of slowing down our party life in order that we build a healthier relationship and life, but invariably every weekend brought with it a reason to celebrate. Now at the end of these nights, Mira and I were together. We spooned each other tightly as the room spun around us. We held on until our respective coma collected us. I was no longer alone. I had dragged Mira down to my level.

Slowly but surely, the parties escalated and so did the alcohol, the lack of sleep, and the drug use. I no longer went to the gym. I no longer was the first to show up at work. My new career was balancing who I was during the week with who I had devolved myself to be on weekends.

Another Christmas was fast approaching, which meant another Vegas bender to look forward to, but it was no longer enough. I needed to step it up if I was going to reach rock bottom. My body desperately needed to stop, but all I could do was go faster. I needed to submerge myself until there was no chance of resurfacing into the air of real life.

Mira, Brayden, and Paige wanted in on Christmas in Vegas, but wouldn't sacrifice being with their families, something I was too selfish to consider myself. Only Michelle agreed to join me in Vegas for Christmas. Mira and the others planned around their familial obligations of the holidays, and we all decided to up the ante.

Mira, Brayden, and Paige planned to join Michelle and me in Vegas two days after Christmas. We planned to party in the clubs, then we'd all fly to Cabo to spend the next week in a private villa. Another friend of mine dared me to join him on a four-day rave cruise called Holy Ship! that began on the last day of our Cabo stay. This would take my bender to fourteen days, and I would be the only one to be a part of all the activities.

After three drunken nights, Mira and the group joined us in Vegas. While dancing at Tao Nightclub, I told Mira I loved her for the first time. She turned away and continued dancing. I knew she heard me but she didn't respond or acknowledge it. We never discussed it. I took more Molly and speed. We continued the night at Drai's After Hours and the following night, we did it again.

I was thankful to get the reprieve of the day of travel from Vegas to Cabo. Unfortunately, I can't sleep on planes. We landed in Cabo and made our way to the villa, which was located in Pedregal, an upscale, gated community filled with homes with views of the ocean. When we arrived, Brayden set up his DJ equipment and started the music. The music would continue for the duration of our stay and could be heard in each of the six rooms as well as in the infinity pool that overlooked the ocean.

A few of us were able to smuggle drugs into Mexico but decided we would "take it easy" the first night and leave them at the villa. It was an attempt at being responsible. I was torn on this decision. On the one hand, the break would give my body a chance to recover. On the other, the comedown would be harsher than I had ever experienced given that I hadn't yet rested my body in the past seven days.

We found a club our first night. When we walked in, the place was empty. I laughed when Brayden told me he found Ecstasy and was buying some. The promoter took a liking to us, in no small part because we had just purchased a bunch of drugs from him. He invited us all to his private table in the DJ booth. In well-known clubs in Vegas, the DJ area is the best piece of real estate in the club. It meant you were a high roller or part of the DJ's entourage, either of which would make you look like someone important. This DJ area, however, was a dark room with a couple of sofas behind where the DJ was playing. Hidden from view from the rest of the club, anyone inside it could imbibe as many drugs as they felt appropriate. The promoter handed each of us a pressed tab of Ecstasy. I took two.

Brayden made friends with the DJ while I stared, entranced by the lights from the mixers as I waited for my new high to kick in. It occurred to me that all the music we listened to in clubs sounded the same. Nonetheless, I always smiled excitedly when Brayden pointed to his ear, indicating I should listen carefully as he tried to explain what the DJ was doing to produce the music. I never knew what he was talking about but I was too embarrassed to admit it. I also didn't want to ruin his fun.

As I started to yawn from the exhaustion, my medicine kicked in. It had been a while since I had taken a pressed pill of ecstasy. I'd forgotten about the first wave. The glorious embrace of the warmth worked its way up from my ankles through my spine and into my retinas. My pupils widened; my knees buckled. I found my way to a free seat on one of the sofas. When I looked down, I could see the couch was black leather, but the room was so dark and my eyesight so blurred, that I couldn't make out where the seat level was. With one trusted plunge, I dropped backward toward the couch and hoped it would catch me. I fell past where I expected the seat to catch me. My body tried to compensate by straightening out and my hands rushed to stop my fall. My torso, stiff from preparing to fall, struggled to accept that I had dropped safely into my seat. I sat mortified, with my hands still stiffly holding me in place. I took another pill that night, then blacked out from the alcohol. I woke up vomiting in our bathroom at the villa. The music was still playing.

The next day and night continued with much of the same and when we returned to the villa, Mira and I went back to our room. As we laid in bed, I said it again. "I love you."

"Stop saying that when you're high!" She turned away.

Mira was right. Saying those words, especially for the first time, while high had little meaning. I loved anything and everything when I was high. I loved the lint on the thread that secured my belt loops when I was high. Mira's words dissolved the high I felt. Reality set in and it was awful. I was awful. The truth was I did love Mira. Not because of the drugs. Because we connected deeper than the drugs could take us. I caught the looks in her eyes that asked me when these nights would be over, when we could be normal. I looked away. Now I was using the high as both a crutch and as an out in telling her I loved her.

The last two days after New Year's Eve were quiet. Many of the crew struggled to wake up and those who did kept to themselves. The never-ending music was no longer playing. It was time for most of them to go home where they would recover and heal. It was time for me and Mira to fly to Miami for the final four-day leg of our adventure.

The sky spat on us as the cab approached the rusted, weathered cruise ship. I felt my eyes beginning to tear from overwhelming sadness as my body tried to race from the oncoming comedown. It had been ten days since my body had been sober and healthy enough to produce its own serotonin and I worried that it forgot how. We stepped out of the cab into a sea of thousands slowly making their way into a small building through which we'd pass before boarding. After what seemed like hours, we entered the building to see the line split into a half dozen of smaller lines for security. Every checkpoint had drug-detecting dogs stuffing their noses into every piece of luggage and each human. A lightning strike of fear came over me before I realized I had no drugs on my body. I didn't plan it that way. My inventory was merely depleted. I intended to find some on board.

Eventually, we got through security and the maze of tiny hallways, the entrances made even smaller by piles of luggage. We found our way to our cabin, which was intended for three. There were five of us. Mira and I took the floor.

Unsurprisingly, we found a drug dealer and made our purchase. I swallowed three pills anxiously awaiting its effects to numb my aching carcass. Everything about Holy Ship! violently offended my senses. It was not a PLUR crowd, but a fraternity, a Spring Break-like party. The people at this event were looking to get drunk and laid. I could feel the piercing heat of strangers' eyes glare at us. The guys were undressing Mira with their stares while nodding their heads trying to get her attention. I scanned her response and became enraged when she returned a smile. I'd watch her call them over and start a conversation as my stomach unraveled inside. Our friends rolled their eyes and turned away when they saw how uncomfortable I was acting. Kevin just gave me an "I told you so." My chest plate pounded like a subwoofer. My fingers trembled with panic. *What am I doing on this ship? How could I have been so stupid to think someone as beautiful and kind as Mira could be with only me? Why can't I just dance and enjoy the music like everybody else?*

Mira turned to me and grabbed my shoulders. "Are you okay?" Her voice rocketed at me from far away. I saw her eyes inches away from mine. I looked around her. No one was there. She wasn't talking to anyone, nor had she called anyone over. Our friends came close to investigate. None of what I was seeing was happening. When they approached, I couldn't focus on any of their faces. My eyes were circling frantically and I couldn't breathe. Mira sat me down on the ground. My heart raced while I tried to tell her I was fine. I didn't know if I was dreaming or if they were playing a cruel joke on me. My mood changed to anger. I stopped trying to explain myself. I jumped up and decided I would force my body through the rest of the trip. If I was lucky, my body would give out.

I joined the crowds jumping and thrashing to the angry sound. Kevin was dancing with me. There was nothing else he could do. In fleeting sober moments, I realized that I was losing my grip on reality. I didn't know if I was happy or angry or depressed or jealous. Truth was a dream. And I couldn't hold on to dreams. Reality was no different. Up and down became a judgment call.

I was sure Mira would never speak to me again once we got home. I was sure my partners would shun me at work. I was sure my mother never loved me. All I had was Kevin and he wouldn't let me die.

On the final day, a few hours away from port a voice came over the loudspeaker. "If you have drugs, do them now." It was the last day of the cruise. I had been high for fourteen days, and all I wanted was to be alone. Mira all but carried me down the narrow stairs of the filthy ship. The same lines formed in reverse, including the dogs. I wondered how much more I could do before my body revolted, forcing me into a coma or, better, a flatline. Sadly, I had no more drugs and even if I did, I was too weak to fight with Mira who insisted she wouldn't let me take any more.

It took weeks to recover, but somehow I did. At work I had gone from marginally competent to aspiring to be marginally competent to struggling to be present. I was received with silence. Meetings that couldn't run without me no longer required me. I sank deeper and immersed myself in menial tasks that could help my staff. Every night I drove home defeated, but I knew that come Thursday a new high would begin, one more escape.

Eat. Sleep. Rave. Repeat.

Unsustainable

"THIS ISN'T FUN ANYMORE." MIRA CONTINUED GAZING AT the ceiling as we lay in bed, still spinning from the past two weeks' binge. Outside, the snow intensified the morning sunlight piercing its way through the curtains like a thousand tiny spotlights.

"I know," I said softly.

"It was glamourous for a while, like in Vegas and all the traveling, but it's all so repetitive. I feel sick all the time now."

"It's totally the same."

"What if we could stop? We can relax and be normal, be..." Mira turned to wrap her arm across my chest.

"Boring?" I offered in the pause.

"Yeah, boring. Can we be boring?"

"Boring sounds pretty nice." The idea of sitting still long enough to be boring threatened me. I turned to Mira and kissed her. "Let's try to be boring."

Mira's expression turned to contentment as she contemplated our future. She was right, and I wished things were different, but I couldn't stop. And when I couldn't stop, Mira couldn't either. Every Thursday we needed the escape. Every Sunday the music ended so abruptly our ears rang throughout the day. Our shared samsara.

Every weekend brought with it a depressing story. Like the time I decided to take GHB and cocaine with my Ecstasy, then feeling the blood roll down my chin from sucking the skin off my tongue. Or when, after a four-day bender, I woke up to Mira screaming my name while I lay on my bathroom floor after passing out and hitting my head on a metal bar. We rushed to the hospital only to scurry away after seeing a doctor and telling him about the drugs. Or the time at an after-party at my condo we accidentally set our neighbour's balcony on fire burning the entire side of the building. Or the time Mira and I went back to EDC only to have our bodies shut down after one night and lay violently sick in the hotel room for days. Or the time we went to New City Gas then straight to Underground then back home to change, re-up on drugs and straight to a Beach Club which was an all-day event. Being unslept, unkempt, and unprepared for the sun resulted in a second-degree sunburn that took weeks to heal. Or the time Mira and I decided to take all the drugs leftover from those we smuggled into the Bahamas the night before our morning flight, and ended up passing out on the airport floor. Or the time Michelle and I decided to do the same in Vegas, only to find the airport floors weren't even and, humiliating our friends, fell to the floor while desperately reaching to hold onto the seats in the terminal.

One night in Ottawa, I was out at a club when I bumped into Moe, the one who introduced me to Gerome. I hadn't seen Moe in a while and the first thing he said was that it was too bad about Gerome. I asked him what he meant, and he was surprised that I hadn't heard. Gerome had been arrested for armed bank robbery along with Sonny. Apparently, they, along with two others, were known to police as the Sledgehammer Gang, a moniker signifying the chosen method of entry into the bank right before opening. Once in the bank, they robbed it at gunpoint. They had hit seven banks and gotten away with over six hundred thousand dollars.

Sonny met me for breakfast one morning after, unbeknownst to me, one of those heists. This breakfast stood out to me for a few reasons. We weren't in the habit of hanging together outside the club scene, and yet I quite enjoyed our exchange over breakfast. To me and my friends, Sonny was a just a big softy. To anyone who didn't know him, he seemed a threateningly violent guy that you wouldn't want to be around. During the breakfast, Sonny and I talked about life and happiness. He gifted me a baggy full of Ecstasy along with a hug, insisting it was because I'd been so nice to him. He said he really loved my friends and how positive we all were. I remember thinking he wanted to get out of the situation he was in and possibly live a normal life. I had no idea he had just come from robbing a bank at gunpoint.

It turned out that the loan-sharking scheme was a farce all along. Gerome had been in debt with even more fearsome men than he, people I was fortunate enough to never meet. Our business was a Ponzi scheme. He was paying me with money he borrowed from other people, one of whom I had brought in. I couldn't even break the law properly.

I didn't care that the business didn't exist. I didn't care about the money. I yearned for the confidence reaped from the power, or at least the appearance of power. Aside from introducing and possibly dealing drugs—in the sense that I would buy large quantities knowing my friends would want some—I was no more of a gangster than a stick bug was a stick. I wore the uniform but I was still an insect. I wasn't even a tourist. Like the rest of my life, I was a fake husband, a fake entrepreneur, an impostor. I was a cardboard cutout of a human and I couldn't wait to die.

How to Lose Friends and Reject People

MIRA AND I TRIED TO SLOW DOWN, BUT IT WASN'T enough. Instead of stopping completely we elected to be selective with whom we spent time. Unfortunately, the people we chose were either in the same situation or could handle getting high without the repercussions. In short, the drugs continued.

In my nonstop lifestyle I was now living, I had severely tested the limits of long-term friendships. There was no time for camaraderie with meaning, or discourse, or even joy. The only people I wanted to see in my life were those with the same addictions, the same loneliness, the same self-delusion. "It's difficult to recognize you have a problem when people with the same problem surround you," said David Clark in his memoir, *Out There*, but this seemed to be what I wanted. To be present with someone who was real and honest would mean I had to admit I had a problem. Unfortunately, Mira fell into the former category, a place into which I knew I had dragged her.

My friendship with Joey was a devastating casualty. Joey and I swam with Great White Sharks in San Francisco together, travelled across Canada in a dilapidated U-Haul, and drove for ten days through New York, Kentucky, Ohio, and Tennessee with no set destination in mind. We just drove. As he was someone I respected, Joey was the first person after Perrine I told about the memory of the rape.

I let Joey down on two occasions. The first was when he came into town with his new girlfriend, and he was going to spend time with me while she visited her friends. We went to a club with an unlimited supply of liquor, girls and music, followed by the customary overnight after-party. This was the very thing Joey and I used to ridicule years earlier. The thing with Joey is that although he was vastly intelligent, witty, and very successful, he was humble. He didn't need the after-work bottle service at a club like his executive colleagues, who brandished over-priced suits and peacocked themselves to impress each other and the waitresses who delivered the bottles. Even though Joey wasn't into drugs of any kind, we badgered him to try some for hours, and finally, at the after-party, he succumbed to the pressure and swallowed a pill. Not too long after, his words slurred while his legs faltered with every step. We giggled and gave him water. When there were only a few of us left, we lay on the floor to stare at the melting ceiling. When Joey woke the next morning, he continued to have trouble speaking. He was dizzy and nauseous when his girlfriend picked him up. We never spoke of it.

The second occasion I let him down was his birthday which was not long after our after-party adventure. Joey had given plenty of notice and invited a bunch of us to camp at his new home. As it approached, I knew I wasn't going to go. "Don't you back out on me!" I assured him I wouldn't. I did. I don't even remember why. I felt awful, and when I sent an apology, I received no response. I was de-friended with good reason. I chose not to pursue it further. As a friend, I had nothing to offer. I could have reached out and asked for help as he once did for himself. I could have done a lot of things better. I don't have a lot of regrets, but I regret letting that friendship go. When thoughts or memories of Joey came up, it only exacerbated my self-hatred. It reminded me I was still not a whole person or even a remotely good one.

I lost contact with other old and loyal friends who wanted no part in what I was doing, and I equally wanted no part of seeing how they would look at me. It wasn't the judgment I feared, rather it was their eyes filled with sadness and pity. They'd likely try to help me, and if that happened, I'd have to admit that I had a problem. I'd have to acknowledge I had no self-control or self-respect to men I loved, respected, and even revered. That window was gone by now. They were gone.

There were countless events I could call my rock bottom, but what happened with Paige at one of our after-parties topped that very long list. Paige and Brayden were in attendance along with a dozen or so of other club acquaintances. On that particular night, I was no longer weighing and capping my own capsules, opting instead to eat or snort the MDMA crystals themselves. The crystals tasted like electric coppery mold and burned my sinuses, but I wanted to get high as fast as I could. I'd also upped my drinking game, which further impaired any ability to gauge how high I was getting. As the music played and everyone laughed, I made my way to Paige who greeted me by wrapping her arms around me as she always did. We were all physically affectionate with each other. We trusted and cared for one another. Deep in my inebriation, I was a different person, however. When Paige put her arm around me, my hand clutched her butt from behind, hard. She laughed as if I was playing a game and I looked at her. She saw that something was wrong and pulled me aside to see if I was okay. I pulled her close and tried to kiss her. Paige examined my expression as she quickly pushed me away. "What are you doing? What's wrong?" I backed away and tried to make sense of what had just happened. I couldn't. I looked around not recognizing my own home. A wave of guilt overwhelmed me. Paige went over to Brayden to tell him what happened and he came over to me.

"Dude, what the fuck?" Brayden's eyes were wide

with rage, his breath quickened. I couldn't answer. "Rob, something is wrong with you right now, and I don't know what it is but you can't just kiss Paige!" I tried to say that I knew that. I tried to say that I was sorry. Nothing came out. Brayden walked me back to my sofa where I slumped back with my eyes rolled up into my head. Paige and Brayden left. The others followed suit, leaving just me and Mira. When I was able to, I spoke.

"I tried to kiss Paige." I didn't look at Mira. I was still on the sofa where Brayden left me. It was beginning to feel like the conversation I'd had with Perrine when we broke up. I had no defense, no words. All I could say was that I was sorry.

"Are you in love with Paige?" Mira asked pointedly.

"Not that way, no," I answered.

"Do you want to be with me and was that just you being drunk and fucked out your mind?" She was giving me an out.

"Yeah." I stared at the ground and took deep breaths. "I'm not sure what's wrong with me. I have no idea why I did that." I was being honest. I didn't know why I did it and this is what scared me. "I am so sorry." I finally turned to Mira who studied me closely.

"I'm glad you told me right away," she said, accepting my apology. "We have to stop partying. I don't know how much longer we can do it."

The next morning, I was sicker than I had ever been. I vomited for hours and when I wasn't kneeling in front of my toilet, all I could think of was what I had done. I remembered my actions vaguely but was frightened that I could do such a thing without having a conscious intention. If I could do something like that, what else could I do? How bad could it get? It wasn't who I was or who I ever wanted to be, and yet it happened. I had now ostracized two people I had grown remarkably close to, and pushed the limit of my relationship with Mira. There were fewer and fewer people in my corner.

Mira lay on the sofa recovering from her night while further contemplating my actions and what we should do. When I finally made it over to her, she proposed her solution. "We need to stop cold turkey." Her eyes focused firmly on mine. She clutched my hand. "No more parties, no more birthdays, no made up bullshit club anniversary parties, nothing." We just needed to stop. "If we can make it through the next weekend, we can do it all weekends. It doesn't have to be forever. We just need to prove to ourselves that we can do it." Was it true? All we needed was to know that we had the willpower to say no and stick to it? If we had that, we weren't addicts. We could even do drugs again at some point and not fall in too deep. It was a great plan.

Despite my mental absence, the company my partners and me had founded was building momentum. We needed to continue to grow but we didn't know how. Mitchel befriended and brought in a well-known venture capitalist, Aaron, to be our CEO. Every interaction with Aaron felt like an inquisition. In my constant state of recovery and the resulting loss of self-confidence and brain cloudiness, I was perpetually defensive. Aaron was an analyst at heart. He studied things and people closely. His threatening intelligence, coupled with seemingly limitless confidence, kept me apprehensive. Any attempt at discourse or even a friendly chat invariably ended with Aaron walking away perplexed. One afternoon he invited me to dinner. He said he wanted to get to know all three of the founders individually.

I met Aaron at the Shore Club steakhouse in downtown Ottawa. We sat at a booth near the back affording us a bit of privacy in that well-known restaurant. "Tell me about yourself, Rob." Aaron never wasted time. "I know about how this company got started, but I want to learn more about your history." Aaron looked at me intently, waiting for my answer. I gave him the Coles notes, but it seemed he already knew where he wanted to take the conversation.

"...and then I met Mitchel and the rest is history," I ended.

"And what about now?" Warning shot received.

"Now I'm working as hard as I can to learn how to manage a bigger team ,and trying to keep the product stable." It was a vague answer. Aaron was about to speak but I interrupted him. "And I know that lately I've been struggling. I'm kind of working through some personal stuff, but I am at the office as much as I can be and the team is doing well." The admission seemed to dissolve the palpable density of the air. We both knew that I hadn't been present, that I was growing ineffective, that I may not even be qualified to be there.

"Answer me honestly. Are you fully in? Are you in it to win it?" The cliché interrupted my train of thought. I sat back in my seat to digest the question. The waiter came for our order. Aaron opened his menu for the first time, and quickly pointed to his favourite steak and ordered a glass of red wine. The waiter turned to me.

"I'll do the same. And a Caesar, with gin instead of the wine." I needed a drink. The waiter walked away. Aaron's eyes fixated on me.

"I am." I looked back at him directly. He continued to study my expression. It occurred to me that Mitchel and Jordan had never broached their concern of my truancy with me directly. It was clear to me now they were not only aware of it, but troubled by it. Secretly my delusion hoped they hadn't noticed, but here it was sitting right in front of me in the form of a no-bullshit CEO. "I've lost their trust, haven't I?"

"It's not that far gone, Rob. Founders go through challenges. I've seen it a hundred times." Given his acumen, I doubt he was exaggerating. "It's clear that you're capable. They just need to see that Rob again." *That Rob? What Rob? I don't remember who "that Rob" is. The guy shackled to his computer twelve hours a day for months, straining his marriages and relationships? That Rob has left the building.*

"I'm not sure how..."

"You show up. Every day. And get some wins. It doesn't matter how small. Get a few victories under your belt and the trust will come." I soaked in the simple advice. My mind scanned the catalogue of challenges my team had been going through to find some we can solve and cry victory. I went home refocused. I was going to make this right before I died. I crafted a list of hurdles to overcome to prove to my partners that I was "in it to win it." Then maybe, I could rest in peace.

The Consummate Professional

AFTER WE WERE ATTACKED AT THE BEACH IN HAMILTON, Gianna and I moved back to Ottawa for her second year at university. We broke up not too long after. The retail jobs I was working gave me enough to rent a place with a roommate. The jobs were very low paying, but I was able to be more social. Most of the jobs I'd had until then were in kitchens washing dishes or cooking, but retail forced me to interact with people every day. I worked at a few cafes and jean shops, but I made a home at Foot Locker.

I wasn't hesitant to work sixty, seventy, even eighty hours a week in the store, and my bosses weren't hesitant to let me. For as long as I can remember, I have always been a dedicated and diligent worker. Be it scummy restaurant dish-pits, dark early-mornings in the cafes, or under the buzzing fluorescent lights of mall retail stores, work was always a solace. Work kept my mind occupied, facing away from what it could have been facing. Work was a welcome deterrent from becoming whole. Work was my drug of choice, and Foot Locker was where the addiction took a firm hold.

I discovered that I was a talented salesperson in my early retail jobs. It was as if my life leading up to working in sales had been preparing me. Salespeople offer who they are in the moment to build a rapport and gain trust quickly. I'd been honing the ability to hide who I was and how I felt inside for years. I longed for everyone, anyone, to like me, so I strove to be jovial whenever I could. When required, I could be charismatic, confident, and affable upon meeting someone new. Couple my manufactured-on-demand charm with my desperate inability to sit still and you have a country-leading salesperson (two years in a row!).

The success I enjoyed at Foot Locker brought with it kudos from my peers who also became friends. It also brought with it my first taste at making "real money." I crossed the thirty thousand dollars a year threshold. This meant I could afford to purchase my own bed (I was sleeping on a mattress made of sweaters on my bedroom floor) and it also gave me a modicum of confidence. I'd left my arrest and attack in Hamilton behind me. I was becoming a real person through the sheer perpetual motion of work.

The success, or possibly the kudos and money that came with it, made me thirsty for more. I learned and enjoyed programming in my early teens while playing with my father's computer, so I felt the field was worth pursuing. I signed up for night courses at Algonquin College, but balancing jobs and school proved difficult. At the busiest time, I started a shift at a cafe from five until eight in the morning, then dashed through the shopping mall to work at Foot Locker until six in the evening. Then I'd take the bus across the city to my programming course, which started at seven and ended at ten. I'd repeat this routine three days a week, studying on the weekends.

Computer programming turned out to be a perfect fit for me. I was able to focus on writing code without having to be around other people. I sat for hours alone typing away, confident that I was accomplishing something. I found a programming job at a local design shop, iHelp Solutions Inc. The company was small—as in I was the only employee. The owner, Gabe, had ambitions to grow over time, but he didn't really know how.

I can attribute my love for boxing for most of my financial success. After joining my local boxing club, I'd become friends with people who helped build my company. One of these was an executive from a large telecom company who gave me a chance to develop for free some software for his team as a sort of audition. Gabe gave me permission to do this on my own, as he felt free work was a slippery slope and didn't see it as an investment. It marked the beginning of my own business.

As iHelp began to struggle, I offered to buy Gabe out.

He agreed and I went into deep personal debt to pay for it. I'd love to say I had a plan but I didn't. I had a handful of small clients, but the income from that work barely paid my overhead. I experienced overwhelming stress finding new clients because I had no idea how to find them. I renamed the company 10Count, an homage to my love for boxing, and was now in business.

The first year was fraught with a constant barrage of challenges. I was developing during the day, and networking, marketing, and doing the bookkeeping at night. Other than programming, I had no idea how to do any of these other things. The company I had developed software for free continued to use us, and we were building on the good name we had with them. By the end of the first year, they had given us over a half of a million dollars, with plans to grow the following year. I hired another developer friend who was an incredible talent. The second year, we nearly doubled our revenue but it was still from the same client. But I'd clawed my way back up to zero, which was far better than being in debt.

I made another contact at the boxing club that would forever change my life. While in university, Mitchel started his own boxing club as well as a technology company, and was looking to grow. Mitchel and I joined forces. While our small companies continued to thrive, we developed another piece of software that took off like wildfire. It spun off into its own corporation, becoming much larger than anything Mitchel and I'd done up until that point. We named it Assent Compliance. Assent was the brainchild of Mitchel's roommate Jordan, who gave me the blueprints upon which I was able to build the software. When Assent began to take off, we managed to procure some top talent and, with the addition of Jordan, all three companies were firing on all cylinders.

After the first year of Fight for the Cure, The Cancer Foundation approached me to serve on their board of directors. The Foundation hoped I would be a unique fit, bringing a fresh young perspective to the mature fifty million dollar organization. In the same year, the Foundation's chairman of the board of directors nominated me as a Business Journal's Top Forty Under 40 recipient, which I was awarded at an event held that summer. At about the same time, I bought a Lamborghini but felt so guilty about buying it, I decided to donate the amount I'd spent on the car to the Cancer Foundation. A year later the Cancer Foundation invited me to meet the Queen at a ceremony held in the Governor General's Garden and in the presence of Prime Minister Stephen Harper. I'd gone from sleeping on a mattress made of sweaters to meeting the Queen of England and the Prime Minister of Canada, not to mention having driven there in a Lamborghini.

From the outside, my life appeared as if I was a successful entrepreneur who had his shit together. It was far from the truth. At home, I was lonely and unhappy. I was cheating on my wife every chance I could, only to feel even worse. I was continually spending more money than

I made and only built a facade of success. Relieving the stress around money only served to reveal the underlying anxiety and fear rooted deep inside me.

I busied myself with work and registered to take university classes, thinking maybe all I needed were more challenges. I studied philosophy and world religions looking for answers, but all it did was preoccupy me more. I turned to seeking out new experiences. I put together a "bucket list" of things to experience before I died.

I tried skydiving and understood why this was a passion, even an addiction. Skydivers jump out of a perfectly good airplane to put themselves in mortal danger. They taunt death. They dare it to try to take them, and although they know they've done everything possible to mitigate the risk by folding and packing the parachute precisely, double and triple-checking every clip, harness, and stitch, there is still a chance they might die. Their bodies respond accordingly with a tremendous boost of adrenaline and dopamine, chemicals that intoxicate. The high doesn't last very long, and so they want more.

Skydiving brought with it something more than what I'd experienced boxing. Boxing, at times, was a punishment. The worst I could get in the ring was beaten up, and maybe I wanted that. Perhaps, I felt I deserved it. With shark diving and skydiving, I was tipping my toe into a different danger. I taunted death more. I mocked death more. Teasing death made me high.

Kevin didn't like that I was facing my fears, but his

voice was fading. He kept quiet as long as I didn't dig too deep. And as long as I didn't dig too deep, I'd always have Kevin. I wasn't ready for him to be gone.

Mira

MIRA SUGGESTED WE TRY MEDITATING. I WAS SKEPTICAL but I downloaded an app, Buddhify. We decided to play a five-minute meditation while in bed before we went to sleep and another when we first woke up in the morning. That night in bed, Mira started the session. A soothing man's voice started whispering. The peaceful calm in his voice allowed me to unclench my body, myself. I let go if only for a few seconds and sleep took me.

The next morning as we lay in bed, Mira stopped me before I tried to slip away so we could listen to the morning meditation. Assuring me that it would only take a few minutes, she started the session. I laid back in bed and set down my phone. A woman's voice began speaking softly in a kind, British accent. The meditation, titled "Good," intended to help the listener start the day off with positive intentions. I rolled my eyes and took a deep breath. *I'll just sit back and relax until this is over, which will make Mira happy.*

"Everyone ultimately just wants to be happy and well." *No shit.* "So often we can sabotage ourselves with self-criticism and feelings of unworthiness, guilt," whispered the woman's voice. "So, by taking a few minutes here to set a positive intention, it can serve as a foundation for the rest of the day. Before the other negative stuff can take hold." *This can't be that bad.*

"We'll do this by repeating some simple phrases." *Here we go.*

"May things be good today," she said. I snickered quietly.

"May things be good today." *I hope Mira is enjoying this.*

"May things be good today." Is she talking to me? My day is another workday. I'm sure my day will be fine, even though I have to deal with hiding the fact that I'm going through a comedown again and I can't focus.

"May things be good today." It hasn't been going well so far. I can't even get around to killing myself. Maybe if I did, it would be a good day.

"May things be good today." Why is this woman saying this? I don't deserve for things to be good today. I deserve whatever is coming to me. I've earned the torment of guilt and shame that hits me like ocean waves over and over again and settling only to make sure I was still barely above water.

"May things be good today." *Stop it!*

"May things be good today." I could barely hold in the tears. Anne would have been proud. She wanted me to cry.

"May things be good today." What would happen if I tried? What would happen if I selfishly took a day away from the misery?

"May things be good today." *I give up! May things be good today.* I whispered in unison with my new friend's voice. The more I repeated it, the more I wanted to have a good day. It didn't matter if I deserved it. I was exhausted. I selfishly wanted a good day. Fuck the guilt! Fuck the shame! Give me this one day. The track ended, but not before one more phrase from my new best friend.

"And if things aren't so good today, may my ability to deal with them be good today." I flashed a smile at Mira and escaped to the washroom to breathe in solitude. The mantra echoed in my brain. I had a good day that day.

It'd been almost two years since I tried to hang myself, two years since I'd made the decision to end my life. I'd been cowardly using drugs and alcohol to avoid going through with it. By this time my savings were depleted, and I'd started amassing credit card debt. Worse still, Mira was giving me hope. I didn't want hope. Hope leads to suffering and I'd had enough suffering. On top of that, my first company had suffered a significant security breach jeopardizing my biggest client who sought to fire us completely. My partners gave up on me at our current company, and I was quickly ostracizing all the people in my life who stood by me. It was time to end my life.

"We have to break up," I said to Mira one night as we were about to go to bed.

"What? Why?" I could hear her breath quicken.

"You know that we're no good for each other." Tears rolled down Mira's cheeks.

"You don't want to work on it? We can have a baby if you want." She reached for my hand.

"We're each other's enabler at this point." My eyes caught hers and I turned away in shame. "And I don't want kids." I sat on the edge of the bed expressionless. I never knew what more to say in these situations. I usually kept quiet, which made things worse. After an awkward while of me sitting there, Mira composed herself. I heard her take a deep breath.

"I know you're right. It just sucks, you know?"

"Yeah." It was over.

"I can move out this weekend, if that's okay."

"Okay."

"Can we still be friends?"

"After some time." After some time, I'll be dead.

"I love you."

"I love you, too." Mira laid down in bed and cried herself to sleep.

The next night we decided to go out for dinner. A goodbye date. We dressed up for what figured to be our last meal together in the historic downtown steakhouse where we'd come to celebrate relatively modest accomplishments like not drinking all week or another A on one of Mira's essays.

"So this is it." Mira smiled with watery eyes. "I think

this breakup will be good for both of us. I need to sober up and finish my degree." Her optimism stung like tiny daggers piercing my skin. I was reminded of our first conversation about philosophy lying in bed. I nodded my head. "You may want to take a break too. We got high way too much. I feel I need to heal my way back to normal." Despite dragging her down to my level of drug use, getting in the way of her progress, and breaking up with her, she still cared. As I looked over at Mira with sober eyes, and realized I really could be in love with her. Sadly, circumstances were the same—actually worse. I already knew I had little to offer as a boyfriend. What was worse was that I cheated on her before we broke up. I sat there steeped in guilt exponentially amplified by the fact that I knew I couldn't go back to her and if I did, I'd have to tell her. I didn't deserve her anyway. I needed to be put out of my, and everyone else's, misery.

To let Mira move her things without me in the way, I booked a trip to see the Toronto Ravers with Brayden. The plan was to visit them for one of their birthdays and not get high. The flight was early in the day on a Friday. It was overcast, and it was difficult to smile. When I powered up my phone after we landed, I'd received dozens of messages from Mira. She'd found out I had cheated on her. My stomach sank as the guilt sunk in. If it was about wanting to sleep with someone else, I could've waited until we had broken up. I knew better. I did it to make sure I went through with breaking up with Mira. There was no way back.

I reread the messages. The first one began with, "I can't believe what Paige just told me was true." After I cheated, I confessed to Brayden what I'd done but was going to make it right by breaking up with Mira. He told Paige and in Paige's hatred for this kind of betrayal, she informed Mira. When we arrived at the ravers' house, the whole gang was quiet. They had all heard. Humiliated, I tried to leave, but Brayden wouldn't let me. I apologized to everyone and kept quiet most of the night. I drank as much as I could.

I awoke to more texts of bewilderment and anger from Mira. Jen, the woman I'd cheated with, was also in Toronto that weekend. I'd met her at an EDM event about a month earlier. She was nineteen-years-old and a cousin to a friend of ours. When I met her, she was high on MDMA for her first time. At some point, Jen had taken my phone under the guise of taking photos and texted herself from it.

"You have my number if you guys want to meet up later," she'd said that night, her eyes unsubtly flirty. Taken aback by her haughty conceit, all I could do was smile. The MDMA in my system told me I liked the idea of being with her. We began texting and agreed to meet at my condo a couple of weekends later, while Mira was away. Sleeping with Jen led to the loss of any possible amicable breakup between myself and Mira, as well as losing the person I believed was my best friend, Paige. The only thing to do now was to get high. I decided to drive home from Toronto with Jen, who also lived in Ottawa while Brayden flew back alone. We both got high while we drove the five hours home.

The weekend after my breakup with Mira, I made my way to Underground to meet Jen again. When I got there, her friends wanted nothing to do with me. Jen chose to leave her friends and we continued the night together, finally leaving at seven in the morning. A friend of mine, one who hadn't deserted me yet, was driving that night and Jen and I lay in the back seat together. Jen passed out at the same time my phone started to vibrate. It was a series of very long texts from Mira.

"Hey, I've been thinking a lot about what's happened with us. I'm not upset or drunk or anything. I still love you, Rob. These feelings just don't go away overnight, but I know we can't be together. I still care about you, and I think you need to know that YOU ARE A DRUG ADDICT! Your friends will not say it, as most of them are addicts themselves or they just like using you when you pay for them all the time. You're not a bad person, but you're continuing to sink deeper into your addiction, and you're better than that. That's all I wanted to say. I imagine you're tucked away recovering or still high somewhere, so I'll leave you to it. No need to respond."

I read it over and over again. I cried. No one had said any of these things to me before, except Mira in her subtle ways when we were recovering on my sofa, but I always ignored it. I was using drugs to avoid doing what I had set out to do and kill myself. But it was more than that. If I wanted to kill myself, I should have done it by now. I didn't know what I was doing. Maybe I was getting high to forget about the rape or to take up time while I hoped I'd heal enough to be able to deal with it. Maybe it had started that way, but every time I sobered up, I saw how much worse I was becoming and decided to hide from that too. I was caught in a violent whirlpool barely able to swim while hoping the water would drown me.

Walden

MIRA LEFT THE CITY TO GET AWAY FROM ME, THE DRUGS, and the lifestyle, but we kept in touch. I was deeply confused at Mira's kindness towards me. It was far more customary for my exes to turn vicious and cruel, embodying William Congreve's caution about a woman scorned. Mira had nothing to gain by being sympathetic. It seemed she genuinely cared about my well-being. I didn't deserve someone like her, even as a friend. I missed her. I missed her even more because of her brutal honesty. Honesty about my drug addiction. Honesty about how I used my self-degradation to mistreat the ones I loved. Her bluntness wasn't malicious. She was merely holding up a mirror.

I couldn't stay home lest I fell victim to yet another drug-fuelled weekend. I needed refuge. A Walden Pond of my own. Unimaginatively, I decided that the real Walden Pond would be a good place to start. I figured it would take a day or two to drive to Concord, Massachusetts, to Thoreau's famous haven from a world that no longer made sense to him. The idea of Thoreau's escape germinated in the back of my mind since Russ first introduced me to it in high school. To escape the pressures and influences of society, I sat steeped in my own dystopian community. Walden was the chance to start again with nothing but nature. I would see it with my own eyes.

I left on a Thursday morning to avoid the bullying temptation a Thursday night would present. I'm not sure why but I wanted to see the shitty apartment buildings in Hamilton where I'd lived and been raped. The route would take me through Toronto where Mira was now living. When I mentioned it to her, she asked me to visit.

It had been months since we'd last seen each other. I picked her up outside of her new place, and we went for lunch where she not so subtly asked to come with me to Walden. I wanted this trip to be my own, but I also missed her. She smiled at me innocently. She'd been so kind to me all this time I couldn't say no.

I took Mira to the landmark I set to see in Hamilton. Mira was going to be a part of this perverse part of my pilgrimage. I veered off the highway and turned onto the broken roads beside the steel plants. Many of them had closed down, but the stench remained. It was getting dark, but the summer air felt balmy. The streets still felt very familiar to me, and I found my way to Barton Street. My stomach tightened, my heart joined it, my shoulders raised like a cat catching sight of an enemy. I was getting closer.

As we approached the corner, all I could see was a massive grocery store with brand new condominiums beside them. The filthy, cracked parking lots where I used to play were gone. The buildings I remembered were no longer there. Everything had been gentrified by trendy condos connected to a row of boutique retail shops. My Ground Zero now had a Starbucks.

It made me sad, angry, embarrassed, and hopeful. I was surprisingly upset because although horrible, it was a part of my childhood. I was angry because I felt there could never be closure. I was embarrassed because I wanted to show Mira where it happened. We drove around and I pointed out where the building had been. We sat there for a time in silence while she held my hand.

The next stop on the This-Is-My-Life tour wasn't a stop at all. I explained the story of my arrest when I was nineteen, and how the deteriorating relationship with my mother along with the prospect of going to prison for an extended stay frightened me into running away and sleeping in the street. We drove to the woods I slept in for those few nights. Only a few blocks away from where I'd been living with my mother over thirty years ago, Mira and I landed on an undeveloped patch of forest next to a busy intersection. We stopped at the side of the road beside the wooded land. It was dark, and we could barely see the first set of trees. I explained that only a few feet beyond those trees was a descending hill. The grade of the slope allowed for a safe walk to less than an acre of forest through which a stream ran. I looked at the darkness between the trees wondering if anyone was down there. I sighed and drove away. Mira and I found a place an hour away where we ate together, comfortable in each other's silence.

It took a few more hours of driving to get to a place where we spent the night. It was a barely lit, dank motel not too far from the highway, but far enough that we couldn't hear the cars race by nor would the lights pollute the sky. When we stepped out of the car, we could see hundreds, maybe thousands of stars. We checked in and made our way to our room, one that boasted a view of the parking lot and a ceiling barely high enough to avoid hitting my head when I entered. We both slept deeply and soundly in each other's arms.

The fresh, crisp air of the morning brought with it a sense of excitement, but first, meditation. Mira played a guided meditation as we lay next to each other. My body, confused by the lack of a required post-Thursday-night-tomfoolery recovery period, was charged with hope.

Our destination was only a few short hours away, and I raced towards it. Walden Pond is in Massachusetts, just outside of Concord, pronounced *Concurd* by the locals. It was a sweltering, sunny day as we drove through the main street filled with antique stores, rustic cafes, and shops. We stopped to eat at one of the cafes and perused an antique store before making our way to Walden.

As we approached the Pond, my breath quickened

with excitement. We made our way from the rows of parked cars and public washrooms along a wooded path. Close to the main lot we found a life-sized replica of the house Thoreau built and resided in. Although I remembered the dimensions of the cabin described by Thoreau—ten feet by fifteen feet—it was smaller than I had envisioned. It held a simple single bed, an iron wood-burning stove, a desk, and a couple of chairs. My old high school friend Russ had never visited Thoreau's cabin, but I believed that one day he would. I jotted down a hello, folded the paper, and wedged it into a crack in the cabin. I later told him where it was. As of this writing, he has not yet gone.

Not too far from the replica was a path that led through a woods that opened to reveal what I felt was my Mecca, Walden Pond. My eyes teared, my heart warmed. The water was calm and crystal clear. The pond was surrounded with thick swaths of bright green trees standing on embankments sloping high and low along the edge of the water. I savoured every breath as I watched the surface of the water mirror the sky and trees. I stood in awe remembering every line of Thoreau's writing. *"We need the tonic of wildness...At the same time that we are earnest to explore and learn all things, we require that all things be mysterious and unexplorable, that land and sea be indefinitely wild, unsurveyed and unfathomed by us because unfathomable. We can never have enough of nature."*

We followed the path to where Thoreau's real cabin

stood. Only pillars protruding from the dirt remained. One of them wore a plaque. The dirt foundation of the cabin sat on an embankment overlooking the water. Henry knew what he was doing. I stood breathing in the air Thoreau once breathed, staring at the trees across the water. We made our way to a small lagoon where we laid out a towel and slid into the water. I sunk my head under the surface and held it there calmly. At that moment there was nothing else. There was no pain, no heartache, no club scene, no drug addiction, no judgment, no ego, no life. There was only me in Thoreau's pond. The pond he revered. The pond he loved. I was steeping in something he held dear. At that moment I knew I didn't want to die. I wanted to stop suffering. I was tired and numb from it all. *"However mean your life is, meet it and live it; do not shun it and call it hard names. It is not so bad as you are. It looks poorest when you are richest. The fault-finder will find faults even in paradise. Love your life, poor as it is. You may perhaps have some pleasant, thrilling, glorious hours..."*

This is where I let you, dear reader, down. This is where I tell you that my decision to take my life has changed. This is where I ask for forgiveness and to let you know that when I started writing this, that I was sincere in believing that I was going to end my life. I intended to say goodbye at the end, and leave a note for someone to send to a publisher or newspaper or something. I had to leave everything I had to get here, but I am at the beginning of a new life, and I am going to share with you how I was able to build and merit finding happiness.

For hours Mira and I lay under the Walden sun and swam in the Walden water. We reconnected as we took our time driving back, taking extra days along the way. We decided to get back together, and she would come back to Ottawa. We were going to get better. We were going to stop the parties and start our lives. There were a few challenges to overcome, however. First, we didn't know how to be together without being high and, second, I was still a drug addict. Kevin offered no insight.

Mira did not move back in with me, electing instead for us to restart our relationship. She was entering her final year of university and wanted to complete her degree with the high grades she had achieved so far. We saw each other only two nights per week when we'd go on dates consuming nothing more than a glass of wine with dinner. Mira's plan left me alone on many nights. I took up painting, wrote essays, and contemplated where I wanted my life to go.

Magic Mushrooms on the Wall

AVOIDING THE CONSTANT TEMPTATION OF GETTING HIGH on the weekends proved to be a struggle. Some weekends I was able to dodge it entirely, electing instead to smudge arbitrarily chosen colours of acrylic paint on cheap white canvases. Mira scheduled her shifts at the restaurant so she served on weekends. Weekend shifts meant more tips while affording the simultaneous benefit of being too busy or tired to go out afterwards. Every sober weekend meant a week with more clarity, confidence, and healthier choices, while drug-filled weekends came with the additional cost of Mondays and Tuesdays stolen for recovery, more shame, and junk food.

A drug-filled Christmas in Las Vegas didn't seem appropriate anymore, so I cancelled. Mira spent Christmas with her family, and I stayed home alone on

Christmas Eve. I purchased dozens of blank canvases and painted while listening to documentaries on Andy Warhol, Jean-Michel Basquiat, and Gerhard Richter. I lost myself in making art. I didn't think about being alone on Christmas, and my phone was silent as I dedicated my night to artistic experiment. I made ten paintings and, for the first time, I liked what I'd created. I made art. I was proud of what I had done, an emotion so foreign to me I barely recognized it. I didn't want to overthink it or enjoy it too much. I tried to protect it. To hold on to it, but I didn't know how.

The next morning, I drove to Montreal for Christmas dinner with Michelle. My sister is a talented chef as well as baker, and she spent the day making us a delicious meal. Her boyfriend, Tobias, was there when I arrived but left to have dinner with his family with the intention of joining us later. Michelle and I had drinks with dinner and a few more after we ate. We decided to take a Molly. I was apprehensive, but it was our Christmas Tradition after all. When Tobias returned from his dinner, he popped his pill to join our journey.

Tobias and I got along famously. He was deeply passionate about life, spirituality, botany, and nature. When we got high together, we communicated in a conversational parkour, jumping from topic to topic. One of the issues we landed on that night was drugs. I mentioned that I had never done a psychedelic like LSD or magic mushrooms before, but that I was curious about their spiritual effects. I wondered if they could provide me with answers. I hadn't yet appreciated the irony of thinking that a drug could help treat my drug problem.

"I have some here! Want to try some right now?" asked Tobias excitedly. I wasn't surprised that he had some, but I wasn't prepared to do it right then and there. Then again, I thought, what is there to be done to prepare? It's not like I have to stretch my hamstrings or train for a marathon to do drugs. You just do them. I was also under the influence of Molly.

"Let's do it!" I let out emphatically, yet instantly anxious. Tobias reached into a drawer in his kitchen island and pulled out a baggy. The baggy contained dark brown, dried pieces of mushrooms.

"First thing you need to know is that they taste awful," he warned me as I sat on the sofa beside Michelle. "Don't chew it too much, just consume it and wash it down with your drink." I wasn't worried. MDMA tastes like rusted copper dipped in superglue, and I can down it—snort it even—pretty quickly. Tobias handed me a small piece that fit in my palm. I stared at it. Was this where I was going to find answers? Will this bring me the clarity and wisdom that many claim it does? Michelle refused to participate. When I looked back at Tobias, he had his piece in his hand and raised it towards me motioning that we toast the occasion. We tapped our mushrooms, and I placed mine in my mouth. It was bitter and tasted like mouldy dirt. I chewed it two or three times, preparing the load for consumption, and swallowed. Following Tobias's instructions, I took a mouthful of my rum and Diet Coke and washed any remaining bit down. It was official. A new high was coming to town, and it scared the shit out of me.

Forty minutes later, everything I looked at was backlit with a green hue. I felt the warm contentment of the MDMA but now with a neon glow. I could get used to this, I thought. It was more of a strange amusement park ride than an uncontrollable high. I could see why people said that being out in nature was the right place to take these. It felt natural, normal even. Tobias and I giggled as we stumbled through their condo until I watched him slowly go down on his knees and crawl over to the kitchen island. When he arrived there, he propped himself up against it sitting upright. His head faced the top of the wall, and he smiled with his eyes shut. The condo floor started to lean to one side, and in a panic, I sat down on the floor. When I looked down to my spread-out hands, the ground was gone. I was floating in darkness. I observed a window into Michelle's condo from the outside. It was drifting away. I grabbed for it, but it was out of reach. There was nothing I could do and then I remembered that none of this was happening, it was the mushrooms. The realization changed nothing, except that I felt my hands were still lying flat against a cold surface I couldn't see.

I clutched my eyes as tightly as I could. I was in the same place. I could not turn it off. I looked around and saw stars and planets. When I looked closer, I saw that some of the lights were windows into other places, other lives. Three stars seemed to notice that I had appeared. They raced at me aggressively. I could move my body, but there was no wind, no gravity, nothing to push on, nothing to grab hold of. I tried to turn away, but I could still see them barreling towards me like rockets that have locked on their target.

"Are you okay?" Michelle's voice said from the ether. I was back in the condo beside her. She looked at me worriedly.

"I don't like this," I said. When I closed my eyes, I was back in the darkness. I kept them open as long as I could but I knew what was waiting in the darkness for me. I asked Michelle for another drink and more Molly in the hopes they could override the mushrooms. I drank the drink and swallowed the pill. My eyes dried.

Michelle, who was going through her Molly high, cuddled close. We sat on the floor comforting each other. I was grateful to have her there and too afraid to close my eyes lest the darkness envelop me again. I blinked as fast as I could. My eyes fixated on whatever was around. Exposed pipes ran along the ceiling, as was trendy in that neighbourhood. I marveled at the oversized arched windows that overlooked Montreal's Old Port. I could see Tobias, who hadn't budged the entire time. My eyes caught sight of the Christmas tree. Its flickering lights looked like stars in the darkness and, just like that, I was back in the darkness. I panicked, furiously looking side to side to find the missile-stars. I saw them. Three windows the size of Michelle's condo walls stared at me. Each of them hovered, moving closer and back again, forcing me to look at what was inside, who was inside.

When I looked in the first window, I saw Jen, the woman with whom I had cheated on Mira. Why was I so taken with her? I realized that the truth was I wasn't taken with her. I was drawn to her youth, the idea of going back and starting my adult life over again. I didn't want to grow up and face the fact that I was on my own. It was a recurring theme throughout my life. I went back to a younger girl to pretend I was her age. I could pretend that I didn't have to make the mature decisions that I didn't want to make. I was caught in a cycle and the only thing that came from it was the heartache I inflicted on these girls. I had no business even talking to Jen. What kind of disgusting human was I?

Like a violent old rollercoaster, my body jerked away and was thrust into another window. It was Perrine. I could see her as I first saw her, tickling her client who was dying of MS Duchenne, while he laughed softly and scolded her. It was the moment I fell in love with her. I felt a knife pierce through my chest. I screamed. Perrine heard me. She looked at me and cried as she did on the sofa when we broke up. Looking up at me her eyes turned and the knife began to burn. "I wish you really *did* commit suicide! You are so disgusting!" The words broke my heart all over again. I tried to claw my way out of where I was, but nothing I did could stop it. Just then, the pain melted away. I was now walking hand in hand with Perrine at the Biodome in Montreal. We looked into each other's eyes with hope. "Maybe we can fix it. Maybe we can try again. You just have to pass a lie detector test. I have the number." Tears rolled down my cheeks as my body rocked back and forth, back and forth, back and forth. I didn't want to be with Perrine anymore. *I have to let her go.*

Numb, I drifted away from Perrine's window as I gazed at it through tear-soaked eyes. I begged for this trip to be over. I knew there was another place to go. It was as if my entire body was cupped in a giant's hand and was turning me toward the third window toward my partner in crime, Mira. There she was as gorgeous as ever. Her hair glowed as if powered by the sun. She smiled. I smiled back to watch as I handed her a fistful of pills. Her glow dimmed then dissolved into the air. What at first were her healthy eyes squinting from her smile, were now dark circles, her exhausted expression looking at me helplessly. Mira's hands reached to me begging for help. I couldn't reach back. I tried to move to her, but my body pulled away further. What was I doing with Mira? It was bad enough that I was fucking up my own life, why did I have to mess up hers? Mira was an intelligent, kind, beautiful human being who deserves a real shot at life. She doesn't deserve to be swept up in the whirlpool of shit that I created. *I have to let her go too.*

Dozens of other windows hurried towards me. They were the others. All the people I had hurt in my life who wanted to show me how. Sobbing, I begged for them to stop and then I let go. I deserved every one of these, I thought. I prepared myself for the punishment. As they approached, I felt Michelle's hand. It was on my chest and was pushing me awake.

"Hey," Michelle said softly. "Hey," she said a little louder. My heart still raced, but at least I was back in the condo. I sighed in relief, but not too deeply.

"Hey." Michelle's hands wiped away my tears. We said nothing.

I avoided the darkness for the rest of the night and into the morning. I despised the entire experience. It's what people called a bad trip. I wasn't cut out for these drugs. I needed to be alone to recalibrate. Merry Fucking Christmas!

Pivot

STILL HAUNTED BY THE PUNISHING PSYCHEDELIC MUSH-
room experience from Christmas, I prepared for a trip
to the Dominican Republic where Mira and I had volun-
teered to build homes for families in need. I originally
tried to organize the trip with Paige and Brayden, but I
had pushed them enough that they elected to go with
another group. Mira and I left a few days after Christmas, but I was still resolute to keep to the promise I made
in the darkness of my mushroom experience. I had to
let her go. In an effort to stay focused on the volunteer
work, I thought it best to break up with her after we
returned home.

When we arrived in the Republic, ten of us volunteers from Live Different climbed into the back of an
open transport that resembled an extended pickup truck
with a canvas roof. The truck took us to a neighbourhood
called Aqua Negro, meaning black water, where we'd be
building a home. Aqua Negro earned its name from the

black liquid that seeps up from the ground when it rains. The liquid comes from the sediment of a landfill on which the neighbourhood's thousands of "homes" are built. We arrived right after a rainfall. The murky ground was not to be outdone by the stench of damp mold and rotting waste. Pulling your T-shirt over your nose proved futile. After a few minutes, the smell steeped into your clothes. The homes that Live Different was building were on foundations raised above the dark soil, reducing the potential of flooding.

Groups of children swarmed us. They wanted to play with our cell phones, put on our sunglasses, and hold our hands. They were playing, dancing, and laughing. They had so little yet spread so much joy. Every volunteer beamed with delight in every interaction.

We met the families for which we were building a home. They had a young teenage daughter with special needs who was attracted to Mira. Mira was equally drawn to the girl and they spent time together chatting and playing with each other's hair throughout our stay.

Each morning we were driven to the job site where we jumped right into mixing the cement for the day. The foreman instructed us all to encircle a pile of cement mix with shovels. Once we were all in place, buckets of water were poured onto the pile through an assembly line of other workers. Our job was to catch and mix the water with the cement before it made its way to the ground. The mixture became heavier with each drop of water, and the task served as a morning cardio workout preparing us for the day ahead.

The group of volunteers grew throughout the day as neighbours and friends joined the effort. There was no trace of jealousy, rather a genuine excitement that their community was improving. There was a chance, however, these good Samaritans may be eligible to receive a new home themselves. For whatever reason, they worked diligently on every task. As the sweltering sun beat down on us, we shared stories and laughed, and every day ended in sweaty hugs and high fives. We left the job site simultaneously exhausted and energized.

Watching the children, still dancing and singing, wave to us as we left, I was overwhelmed by waves of guilt. The families here lived in houses made of sheet metal, flooded with garbage water, some open to the elements without a fourth wall. Building a home for them did not cost a lot of money. What I threw away in nightclubs and on drugs could have paid for hundreds of homes for people I now considered friends. People with whom I joked and sweated. I could've just donated everything I had, which would have made a positive difference in the world. I needed to change more than I had known.

One highlight of the trip was meeting Cole. Cole was the resident Operations Manager of Live Different in the Dominican Republic and Haiti. He helped build hundreds of homes and schools, and was working on building much more. "Helping people is complicated," said Cole one night to a group of about forty of us exhausted volunteers. I didn't quite grasp the depth of Cole's statement at the time, but in getting to know him and observing the inner workings of the communities and governments involved, I quickly grew to understand.

Cole had walked away from a comfortable life in Canada to help people in impoverished countries, and he had lived with them for over ten years. Community leaders respected him, his staff and colleagues loved him, and the volunteers were inspired by him. On nights after a hard day's work, we enjoyed dinner together and drinks on the beach. Cole brought me to an eerily fascinating abandoned vacation resort. A few pesos over to the security guard and we were off discovering the broken-down staircases and moss-covered suites boasting impeccable views of a lagoon with white sand beaches.

On New Year's Eve, Mira and I had an early dinner and went back to our room. We wanted to avoid any festivities which may tempt us into drinking. We slid into bed and started watching Netflix shows on an iPad. She reached over to hold my hand. I looked down at our entwined hands.

"Are you okay? You seem distant." Mira was right. I knew I was going to break up with her and I didn't want to take advantage in any way. I didn't initiate any physical affection.

"Yeah. I'm okay." I couldn't hide my preoccupation.

"What's going on?" Her hand stopped holding mine.

I didn't want to lie. I took a deep breath and looked into her eyes.

"We have to break up." I didn't look away. For the first time in any breakup, I wanted Mira to know that I was serious and sincere about why.

"I know," Mira said calmly, nodding her head. Her expression showed acceptance and understanding. "I knew this was coming."

"I'm sorry."

"No, no. I get it." We left it at that.

The rest of the trip Mira and I continued as friends. We joked around, slept in the same bed, and discussed strategies on how we planned to go about healing independently. It occurred to me that in the entire ten days in the Dominican Republic, I hadn't wanted to get high nor had I thought about suicide. I was too busy physically working to think about it. What's more, I'd been unable to retreat to the shelter of solitude without panic, without the overwhelming anxiety from the agoraphobia which I believed I suffered. In what little difference I thought I made in the trip, whatever suffering I may have helped remove by providing a home for a family, I healed a tiny fraction of myself.

When I returned to work in the new year, Aaron, our CEO, hired Chase, a consultant friend of his who was also a seasoned CEO, to take a closer look at what I was doing and the team I had built. My group had grown to thirty, and I was trying to manage the product design and software development while also trying to fulfill increasingly more customer requests. The job would be challenging for a sober person, let alone someone with a catalogue of personal issues like mine. Although initially defensive, I decided to leave my ego aside and learn as much as I could from Chase.

Chase spoke almost exclusively in metaphors, most of them comical. He was sensitive to the fact that he was coming in to look at what a founder was doing, which I appreciated and made it even easier to put my fragile ego in a drawer. He taught me about how other companies had achieved the same goals under his tenure. We were able to continue building my team and an entirely new one, while also creating a role where I could contribute most effectively.

We hired Chase outright, and I was to report to him. I didn't care about how it looked to the rest of the company. I needed direction and he provided it. Chase was a challenging man to work for, but his presence reinvigorated the company and I had new responsibilities in an area that I enjoyed.

Feeling renewed and energetic, I strived to improve further. I began reading anything and everything I could get my hands on. Aaron and Mitchel read books in droves, and I tried to keep up as much as I could. My reading and my new focus on work recalibrated how I approached considering whether to go out on customary Thursday nights. *If I go out tonight, I'll be tired tomorrow. If I'm tired tomorrow, I'll be less effective or worse, hungover.*

I filled my days with meditation and work. I filled my nights with painting, reading, and writing. These were my new distractions, but it was different this time. Distraction was no longer about avoiding looking within. I was now deliberately leveraging positive distractions to help stabilize me until I was able to take a closer look. When catastrophic thoughts arose, I took a breath and meditated. I reminded myself the feelings would pass, and they did. I was learning to walk without the crutches of alcohol and drugs. I was learning how to be alone without being lonely.

Some nights went by without incident, other nights temptation set in and I struggled to decline alluring invitations back into the darkness. Most nights I stood firm, most nights.

Meteoric Rise to Zero

EVEN THOUGH I FELT HAPPIER AND ENERGIZED THROUGH-out the day, I yearned to be back in the comfortable agony of depression. The darkness kept calling but its voice was muted, as if from behind a layer of glass and I turned away pretending it wasn't there. I knew I had to confront it one day, but not today. Not for a few todays. Not until I could withstand its assault.

Led by meditation, my daily ritual became the cornerstone of my day. More important than work, more important than sleep. I awoke early every morning to ensure I wouldn't miss it. My newfound regimen meant that if I wanted to get enough sleep, I'd have to go to bed early. Mornings now consisted of a ten- to fifteen-minute guided meditation, a twenty-minute yoga routine via YouTube, and a basic workout including squats, pushups and crunches. I ate a healthy breakfast with fruit, oatmeal, and coffee. I listened to audiobooks and podcasts while eating, but the content was less about work and more about how to live a fulfilling life. I pursued contentment with the same enthusiasm with which I hunted monetary success more than two decades earlier.

In my new sober lifestyle, I reached out to Perrine. I needed to come clean about all the lies I hadn't before. I felt compelled to be honest with myself about the kind of person I was to her, regardless of my past. I did wrong and I had to own it. If I wanted to be an honest person, I had to *be* an honest person, and telling Perrine the truth after denying it for so long was going to be the most difficult thing to do.

"Why now?" Perrine was skeptical. We were sitting on her sofa in her new condo. Rocco, her Silky Terrier and once our dog, sat perched on my lap. He always made me smile. Perrine sat near her balcony door, the sun shining behind her.

"I'm tired of the lies," I admitted. "And you deserve the whole truth." Perrine had been asking me to be honest about who I had cheated with while we were together, as well who I'd had sex with since we broke up. Namely, her friends.

"Marie?" she said, her eyes narrowing. My stomach turned. Perrine had suspected for a long time, but both Marie and I denied it dozens of times. This was by far the biggest test.

"Yes." A wave of heat washed over my body.

"I knew it! Fuck, Rob." Perrine stopped herself to breathe in. "Addison?"

"No."

"Really? C'mon."

"I promise I will never lie to you again." Perrine looked at me skeptically once more. After a few more names, and admissions I had been as appalling an ex-husband as I had been a husband, Perrine took a deep breath. She didn't look at me. She called Rocco over by putting her hand out. He jumped off my lap and into her arms. She kissed him on the head.

"Anything else you think I should know?"

My mind scanned through the worst of it but there was nothing left. "That I'm sorry. I'm sorry I cheated and sorry that I wasn't who you thought I was."

"I thought you were that person because you told me you were, and I believed you."

"I know." All I could see was the floor.

"Thank you for telling me everything."

I smiled an apologetic smile and glanced at Perrine who had turned toward the brightness outside. I turned to the door and put my shoes on. She followed me. When I turned to her to say goodbye, we hugged and held each other. In those breaths we embarked on the long journey to let go of years of lies followed by years of animosity, humiliation, and agony. Averting our eyes, we turned away, and I walked out.

Not too long after, Aaron, my CEO, was getting married and I needed a date. Mira and I were still texting, but hadn't seen each other for weeks. She accepted my invitation to go. Mira showed up at my condo where she changed into a tight red-and-black dress. Her light blonde hair bounced in golden ringlets onto her shoulders. I was still in awe of her, especially when she smiled. We jumped into a cab that took us to the venue, but before we did, I pocketed a baggy filled with Molly, just in case. With all my progress, I still found it hard to stop getting high. It was, after all, a special occasion.

When we arrived at the Fairmont Chateau Laurier, we watched the warm breath leave each other's mouths as clouds of smoke in the frigid air, typical for February in Ottawa. Less than a hundred guests surrounded the couple in a refreshingly unique circular seating formation. After the ceremony, Mira and I made our way to the reception. We were sitting with my partners, Mitchel and Jordan and their dates. The reception played out as most weddings do with a lot of joy, speeches that went too long, awkward silences, and the occasional drunk guest making a spectacle of himself. Mira and I had a few drinks with dinner and as soon as the dessert arrived, we each took a pill. We were together for less than a day, and we were getting high. We didn't care. To us, we proved that we weren't addicts because we hadn't done it in weeks. If this were a diet, this would be our cheat day.

To be as discreet as possible, I reached into my pocket

to take out a pill. When I pulled the baggy out, I tried to open its ziplock but it slipped out of my hands, and the capsules spilled onto the floor right in front of Mitchel. He looked down at the drugs and then back up to me. If Mitchel had Superman's heat vision, a tunnel from my eyes through the back of my skull would have been left in ashes. The embarrassment emanating from my face, or possibly the furious heat from Mitchel's temples, heated the entire reception hall. I had no choice but to get on all fours and pick them up as fast as I could. Mitchel turned away in disgust. Any progress that I had made with our friendship was lost. He walked away, and I decided this would be a good reason to double down on the pills.

After the reception, a bunch of us went to a club where all the same people I had been avoiding welcomed us with big smiles, handshakes, and hugs.

"How are things? Good? Good," said every character with whom I spoke. It was our shorthand. It was as if I had never left and following the tradition of all the other club nights, I decided I would host an after-party just like old times. As the night wore on, Mira and I found ourselves curled up cuddling on our favourite red couch that sat in a far corner of my condo. Although we were high again, we shared moments of clarity, moments of lucidity.

"This isn't us anymore," I said, sighing with a grin.

"No, it isn't." Mira knew precisely what I meant. It was as if we were sitting in a movie theatre watching ourselves on the screen the entire night. Our behaviour, the drugs, the alcohol, the people. The manufactured glee was no longer in charge. We were. Moreover, both Mira and I felt an undeniable connection at that moment.

"The only thing that's stopping us from doing the things we want is us. If we want to make changes, then we make the changes," I said. Mira nodded while we still stared at each other. "I think we should get married," I told her, smiling. The thought had been in the back of my mind for a while, and I believed everything else to be true. Stunned at my suggestion, Mira said nothing. She looked around the condo where huddled groups held their drinks and laughed.

"Are you serious?" Mira inspected my pupils.

"I am," I responded and continued, "We know we love each other. We know each other's dirty secrets, we want the same things, we even travel well together." I liked the idea more and more as I pitched it. "I don't want to party anymore, and I know that I love you and that we can make it through anything if we can make it through this."

"I didn't see this coming. And this is really what you want?" Mira continued to investigate my eyes. I refused to look away.

"It is. I know it sounds insane, especially given that we're high and in the exact place we don't want to be. But we have to move forward if we want to be...boring."

"I like boring." Mira returned a knowing smile. "If we do this, I need some promises."

"Shoot." She was in. My heart started pounding.

"You have to sell the penthouse, and we have to move away from downtown. We need out of this environment." Mira wasn't messing around.

"Done."

"No more drugs for a year. We can reevaluate after that." I was expecting no drugs ever, so this was easy.

"Done."

"For the foreseeable future, no drinking without the other. We need to reestablish our trust."

"Agreed." I couldn't argue this and I didn't want to.

"I guess we're getting married!" Mira whispered. We kissed in private celebration.

We started planning immediately. We agreed to elope, but Mira wanted her parents and sisters to be there. We decided on getting married in Las Vegas in two weeks. We brought Mira's sisters, her parents, my mother, Michelle, and Chowen with us for a secret trip.

When I told Mitchel and Jordan, they were understandingly adamantly against the idea. Both were worried it would end quickly in a divorce, and I was potentially forfeiting millions. I didn't care, but I drew up a marriage contract to appease them. Mira signed it willingly. I had no worries here. Even in our worst breakup when I cheated, Mira was never cruel, vicious or asked for anything.

Lost in the whirlwind of planning our wedding in two short weeks, I avoided speaking with Perrine. I didn't want to lie to her or anyone anymore, and so I told her outright over text.

Me: "Hey, I just wanted you to hear it from me that I'm marrying Mira."

Perrine: "What?? Is this a joke?"

Me: "No, I just decided that I needed to move on with my life and I feel this is the right thing to do."

Perrine: "WTF? She only wants you for your money! You shouldn't do this!"

Me: "I know it sounds crazy, but it's happening soon. I just wanted you to hear it from me. Take care."

Surprisingly, Perrine didn't continue. We didn't speak again.

On February 28, 2015, Mira and I married at the Little Church of the West, the same venue Mira's parents were married thirty-six years before. We managed to arrange a special dedication to them as a part of our ceremony, then celebrated with a dinner at the revolving Top of the World restaurant at the Stratosphere Hotel while the sun set over the Las Vegas strip.

Following our reception, I arranged for us all, including our parents, to go out to my favourite nightclub, XS. I wanted them to see what we were doing when we came to Vegas. I had become friends with the club manager who made special arrangements for our arrival. A dozen glittering, feather-laden showgirls escorted my Mom and Mira's parents arm-over-arm through the club. I leaned over to whisper to my Mom who held my hand, "These girls are here for us."

"No, they're not," she said, dismissing my claim. I

pointed to the giant screen above the DJ stage that read, "Congratulations Rob and Mira" in bright lights. Mom looked at me surprised.

Also surrounding us was my private security. Big Robert had brought his entire staff, whom I'd befriended over the years, as a gift. Every person who was with us was escorted to the dance floor or restroom by a large Samoan bodyguard, who cleared the way through the dense crowd. No one ever had to wait in any line. I wanted everyone to feel special, and only then did I finally understand this was not the way to do it. Mira and I knew that this was a farewell to this lifestyle, and wanted to show the best of it to our family.

Our parents repeatedly asked the name of the famous DJ we saw that night so that they could tell their friends who, of course, would also not know. David Guetta played that night, but all the DJs sounded the same to us by that point. Our parents pumped their fists and danced on sofas in our bottle-service booth, while Mira and I discreetly popped some Molly. We continued to party at an after-hours club after our parents turned in for the night.

It was 9:00 a.m. as we frolicked through the chic, modern decor of the Cosmopolitan Hotel lobby. We bumped into my Mom who was getting a coffee on her way to play the slot machines. She didn't say anything but she knew how we managed to make it through the night. We never spoke of it.

When we returned to Ottawa, I was able to fulfill the

promises I'd made. We bought a house in a quiet neigh-bourhood nearly an hour away from downtown and moved in right away. Not being downtown meant the texts I used to receive at 3:00 a.m. from our nightclub friends to ask to come over ceased. We were no longer tempted by nights out for dinner and drinks which turned into a 4:00 a.m. road trip to Montreal, driving drunk and high on Ecstasy. Weekends in our new home were quiet. Boringly, gloriously, quiet.

Momentum

MONTHS WENT BY WHEN WE DECIDED TO FINALLY HOST a housewarming party. We slipped. We invited people from the bar scene, and as anyone could predict, we got high and drunk with them. The next day, once more, we vowed never to repeat it. Mira and I made a conscious decision to take the drugs that night, and we paid for it through the violent sickness of our hangovers. We didn't let it stop the momentum we had made. We forgave ourselves and each other. That's the big secret. We acknowledged that we as humans are going to fuck up. And we're going to fuck up often, but if we want to move forward, we must avoid getting stuck in the depths of self-hatred. We get back up and try again. It sucks, and it's painful, but this is life. Life is suffering in that it can be inconvenient and presents challenges. It's how we choose to deal with it that defines our character, our happiness, our life.

After the wedding and the house, I was out of money.

I partied my way through everything I had and to make things worse I hadn't paid my taxes the year before. The taxes amounted to a sizable debt to the government. It was as if I was starting over, but fifteen years had gone by. The weight of the debt suffocated me every night. I had to somehow tell Mira that we'd have to sell the house in order to buy one we could afford.

Despite the millions I made over the years, I was now living paycheck to paycheck with no end in sight until an opportunity presented itself. Aaron told me he wanted more "skin in the game" and wanted to invest some of his own money into our company and even purchase some ownership in it. I was forthright with him about my debt, and Aaron offered to provide some relief. He purchased enough for me to pay off my debt. I was now back to zero again, and Aaron was my new partner.

* * *

The summer after Mira and I moved into our new house, we attended a camp for adults called the Good Life Project. The camp was the brainchild of Jonathan Fields with the tagline "Summer Camp for Creative Souls, Entrepreneurs & Change-Makers!" I was apprehensive about being around so many people while sober, but liked the idea of being in nature. There was no alcohol allowed for the entire three and a half days, which was far from the case during weekends at home.

At camp, every morning started with group meditation. After breakfast, a talk was given by a guest speaker who could be a scientist, a TED talk speaker, an author, entrepreneur, or others. Workshops were held on a broad spectrum of fields. They could be entrepreneurial, creative, spiritual, or just plain fun. Every evening after dinner, there was another high-calibre guest speaker who always blew the audience away.

One speaker I was particularly taken with was AJ Leon. AJ was climbing the ladder of success in a Wall Street financial firm, but felt empty inside. After being offered an exciting promotion, a job many of his colleagues would die or kill for, AJ quit. Though the position included generous compensation, what he was doing wasn't fulfilling. AJ left the company with no safety net other than a supportive fiancé, and started a digital marketing company called Misfit. To me, this wasn't about the entrepreneurship. Leon followed his heart above all other priorities. His story resonated with me. My own company had outgrown me. I was contributing, but it was no longer a small, nimble team. It had grown to over three hundred staff and was still growing. I could not continue to do the things I loved doing. At some point, I realized, I'd have to go.

On the last day of camp, I managed to sit down with Jonathan Fields and, although this was his Super Bowl, he gave me his full attention. It caught me off guard, making me nervous about what I was going to tell him. I wanted to share my story with him and how much the weekend meant to me. I wasn't sure where to start and, in my confusion, settled for "Thank you for this." He smiled and shook my hand. He looked into my eyes as if to say he knew I wanted to say more, but I couldn't. Remnants of the drug-inflicted broken confidence still lurked in my psyche.

I continued to move forward and contributed more at work. My commute took much longer now, which meant more time for learning through audiobooks and podcasts. I read before bed and even my morning ritual evolved. I dove deeper, finding meditation techniques profound to me in my developing state. I slowed down, left my phone in my car, and focused on the people around me. Even though I limited the hours of working, they were more productive than if I worked more with less attention.

I began a practice of gratitude which consisted of physically writing three things I was grateful for every day. These could be anything from the profundity of life to the mundane of a good night's rest, or even a soft pillow. I added affirmations to the gratitude, such as, "I love and respect myself," and started to believe them. And if I thought of a reason why I shouldn't respect myself, I changed that aspect of myself so that I could. Slowly, one day at a time, I fought my way back to being whole. I just needed to figure out how to stop drugs and alcohol altogether.

I was working from home one Friday when Jordan

asked if I could host a mutual friend's birthday party. I agreed. Mira was out of town, but due to arrive later in the evening, and was happy to join the party already in progress. I had a few drinks with everyone as they arrived, but waited for Mira to get home to pop some pills together. It had been a few weeks since the housewarming and we'd ignored the promise we made to ourselves. When Mira arrived home, I went over to her, excited for us to get high. Mira smiled and said that she felt tired from the travel and wanted to skip the drugs. She said it would be okay if I did, but I didn't want to be high without her. I had a few more drinks and, uncharacteristically for us, the night ended at a reasonable time. Mira and I stayed awake and cleaned up.

The next morning, we sat at our kitchen island enjoying our morning coffee and appreciating the absence of a hangover. As Mira looked down at her phone I could hear her mutter, "Hmm, that would mean it would be around your birthday." I took out some strawberries and blueberries for my morning cereal and set them down.

"What would be around my birthday?" I asked.

"If I'm pregnant, the baby would be born around your birthday." She looked at me with a smile. I stared back at her, the spoon frozen halfway to my mouth. I stepped into another dimension while my face, my body, my soul smiled uncontrollably. The room got brighter. Life got brighter. I ran to Mira teary eyed and hugged her.

"Are you?" I asked. It occurred to me this was why Mira elected to not drink or drop Molly the night before.

"The two tests I took say I am." In a heartbeat, the world was a different place. There was more joy in me than I could ever have fathomed. Whenever I had considered the moment of hearing I was going to have a baby, I was unsure what my reaction would be. I didn't know if I would be happy or, worse, I feared I would not react appropriately. I worried that whomever was telling me this news would remember my reaction forever. My fears were quelled. I was ecstatic. No amount of drugs or alcohol could come close to making me feel like I did in that moment.

The news of our pregnancy slingshotted the positive momentum we'd built over the past few months. We wanted ourselves and the baby to be as healthy as possible, so we began researching. Instantly, drugs and alcohol were banished from our lives, and so were the people we associated with them. Having already ostracized many of them was a serendipitous irony. We both started exercising regularly, meditating, and sleeping more. I continued to paint and write while Mira started a YouTube channel to share her pregnancy experience.

With every new, positive change I made in my life, I felt renewed. One area I had been curious about for a long time was nutrition. Yet with so much contradiction about which foods were healthy and unhealthy, I decided to find out for myself. The books I consumed every day shifted from business to personal self-improvement to nutrition. Some of these were also confusing and convoluted until I found a source I trusted. When I asked my doctor about nutrition, he recommended reading The China Study. I bought a copy. I took a course that taught laypeople how to properly read scientific studies on nutrition. I read as many studies as I could, but this was still overwhelming. I needed a different approach.

I started treating food as fuel. I wanted the best possible nourishment that would fulfill as much of my daily required nutrients as possible. I dubbed this the "Reverse Diet." Instead of worrying about what to avoid, I focused on what to consume. This also worked psychologically as avoiding food is akin to depriving yourself of food, which felt like punishment. If I focused on how to nourish my body, it meant that I was loving myself. I found lists upon lists of "superfoods" that I assembled and then painstakingly added them to a free online nutrient calculator.

In months of trying to assemble the perfect diet, I noticed that meat was not on any of the lists. The China Study, and the dozens of other studies with data on hundreds of thousands of people, conducted by world renowned scientists—including some Nobel Prize laureates—that spanned decades all pointed to one theory. A whole food plant-based diet was the healthiest diet for humans. I was not a vegan. Michelle had been vegan for years which I teased her about, calling it an eating disability. I even had a fridge magnet that read "Meat is Murder.

Tasty, tasty murder." I didn't realize that, aside from the animals, I was the one being murdered. Even though I felt I loved animals, I made my peace with the fact that I had to eat them to survive long ago. I didn't stop to ask myself why I needed to come to terms with this at all. Why, as a child, was I upset that I had to eat animals? Now the data that I was finding said we didn't need it.

I decided to put it to the test. I had my doctor take a full blood panel and I ate a whole food plant-based diet for thirty days, after which I had my blood checked again. The results were undeniable. My good cholesterol went up, my bad cholesterol—which was dangerously high—stabilized. I lost weight. I had more energy. I was having better sex. I was no longer a high risk for diabetes. I benefited from a host of other improvements, not the least of which was that I felt proud that I was not causing suffering. I was sold, and became plant-based that day and haven't looked back. I posted a blog about it called, "What Does the Blood Say After 30 Days Vegan" which went viral. I thought it would be a good idea to watch *Earthlings*, a documentary about how humans treat animals. After watching the footage, I couldn't sleep for days. It was worse than I imagined. I watched it until the very end and immediately got rid of any animal products in my life. No leather, no wool, cashmere, nothing. I did not want to be a part of any suffering. The decision to go vegan was another step on my path of redemption. I wanted to set the best possible example as a father, and living fiercely with my beliefs was an important part.

Mira and I went out one time when she was six months pregnant. She said I could have a drink if I wanted to join our friends and I did. It wasn't the same. I committed to not drink alcohol both in solidarity with Mira and because I no longer wanted it in my life. Even though Mira had told me it was okay, I still felt I was betraying someone. I was betraying the promise I made to myself, and if you can't keep a promise to yourself then who else would trust you?

Clayton M. Christensen, *New York Times* bestselling author and professor of business administration at Harvard Business School, says in his book, *How Will You Measure Your Life?* "If you give in to 'just this once,' based on a marginal-cost analysis, you'll regret where you end up. That's the lesson I learned: it's easier to hold to your principles 100 percent of the time than it is to hold to them 98 percent of the time. The boundary—your personal moral line—is powerful because you don't cross it; if you have justified doing it once, there's nothing to stop you from doing it again. Decide what you stand for. And then stand for it all the time."

The words seared their message into me like a red-hot brand, and I contemplated them for hours, years. The message was something I needed to hear from my parents, my teachers, anyone, but never did. I decided I would no longer drink alcohol, even after the baby was born and when Mira could. In my mind, I called it "living with integrity," a mantra I would repeat to myself sometimes out loud when I was alone. For months, I meditated on what integrity meant to me.

I'd like to say that I've treated drugs the same way, but I'd be lying. I've had Molly a couple of times, and each time I paid for it with vicious hangovers. Although I don't plan on doing them ever again, it just might happen under the right circumstances.

Drugs and Alcohol weren't the only boxes I needed to check. I promised I would never be disloyal to Mira or anyone else. I vowed to be as honest with myself and others as I could be. I would live a life as a worthy human, husband, and father.

A big part of who I wanted to be was someone that helped people. The memory of building homes in the Dominican Republic hadn't faded, and I wanted to do more. I was still messaging Cole, my friend and Live Different project coordinator in the Republic, and I asked him if there was a project we could start together. He responded immediately.

"Hey, brother! Ya, I've been wanting to start building in an area in Haiti that desperately needs help. It's close to the school we built there. There's a single mother with five boys who really need and deserve a better home."

"That sounds perfect." My heart raced in excitement. "What are the next steps?"

"You can send money as a donation through the Live Different site and we schedule the build. We can do it next month if you want." I smiled excitedly at my iPhone. If anyone had been watching, they'd certainly wonder who I was talking to. I wasn't sure Mira would be able to go to Haiti as she was finishing a postgrad certification, but I thought I could go down alone for a few days to visit the community and Cole.

"That works. I am sending it right now." Even though I was rebuilding my savings this project felt dear to me. I did not want to wait, to consider, to ponder or give any reason to change my mind. I opened my laptop, navigated to the donations page of Live Different website and sent the money. "Done."

"Wow, that was quick. Thanks, Rob, this is going to help an amazing family. I'll message you as soon as we have dates. Can't wait for you to see Haiti!"

A week later Cole messaged me the dates but there was a worldwide epidemic: the Zika virus. Mira was pregnant and the city I was flying into, Cap-Haitien, had reported many cases. I couldn't go for the build for fear of being infected and bringing the virus back to Mira. I was still excited for the project to take place, knowing that I had at least fully funded it, but was disappointed I couldn't be there. I wouldn't get my hands dirty in the sweltering sun. I couldn't meet the family and the community. I vowed to myself, and Cole, to travel to Haiti or the Dominican Republic for a visit when I had the chance.

Cole was understanding when I gave him the news I wouldn't be coming for the build. He assured me that everything was still on schedule, and promised to send me reports of its progress. Cole kept his promise with photos via text message, and when the home was done he narrated a video of the project and the family as a thank you which can be seen on YouTube. I tear up every time I watch it.

It was a cold morning in October when, after showering and preparing for work, my phone rang and interrupted the audiobook I was listening to. A friend messaged me a link to a news article. When I opened the link, the headline read, "Local aid worker killed in plane crash remembered for helping the poor." Cole was in a small aircraft transporting relief supplies to Haiti in the aftermath of Hurricane Matthew when an electrical storm hit. The plane was lost at sea six miles off the coast of the Dominican Republic.

No, no, no, no, no! I texted Cole to ask him if he was okay. *He might be okay. Maybe he's been found and they hadn't yet reported it.* I watched and waited for the magic three dots to appear on the screen signifying that the person on the other end was typing a response. No dots appeared. *I'm sure he's okay. He just needs to rest.* This is what psychologists call denial.

I sat at the foot of my bed, looking down at my phone. The room blurred. Teardrops fell on to my hands. *He's not okay.* I took a few deep breaths. *Thank you, Cole. I'm sorry I missed our meeting. Thank you for a friendship that was far too short. Thank you for inspiring me to be better than I am.*

Cole's death hit me at a pivotal time, but his life deserved to be celebrated and honoured.

In her final semester, Mira registered for a full course load of her postgraduate program in the hopes she would finish before the baby arrived. Her classmates witnessed her belly grow as the weeks passed. Despite the growing discomfort, she missed no classes and delivered her assignments on time. Only two weeks before our due date, Mira completed her final exam and earned her postgraduate certificate.

Vivian

ON A PARTICULARLY BRISK BUT HUMID MORNING IN MAY, Mira was ready to go to the birthing center. We had prepared for this moment and, even though I had been confident in my driving, my hands trembled with anxiety. *How do I drive again? What comes first? Buckle safety belt or turn the car on? It doesn't matter. Is Mira buckled in? Yes, she is. Where are we going? Should I look at my GPS when I'm driving?* "Are we going to go?" Mira quipped between her breathing.

"Okay, sorry. Let's go." I drove unreasonably below the speed limit while Mira focused on coping with her contractions. When we arrived at the birthing centre, a midwife showed us to our room which resembled more of a luxury hotel suite than a hospital room. A large tub, filled and bubbling in the corner, lay only a few feet from a sofa which faced a calming fireplace. A fully motorized, king-size hospital bed lay facing an en suite complete with shower. The luxuries found in our space were comforting, but although every visit, every checkup, every test came back positive, there still existed an undercurrent of apprehension. We were still not in a hospital where, if complications occurred, doctors were physically close to jump on the case.

As the frequency of Mira's contractions increased, so too did their intensity. With each wave of pain, I massaged her lower back with so much force my forearms stiffened. I followed her from the bed to the warm tub and back again. Our midwife paid regular visits to take vitals, warmly asking Mira how she was feeling. Each answer described a more intense discomfort and after ten hours, it was time for the midwife to stay.

After an exhausting twelve hours of contractions at home followed by another ten hours of increasingly severe bouts, Mira sighed in relief that the final process was beginning.

"Okay it's time to start pushing," the midwife said to Mira, before calmly giving me my instructions. I was the cheerleader, the partner, the one to reassure Mira that everything was okay and to motivate her to continue pushing no matter how difficult or how much time had passed. I held her hand as she clutched mine with all her strength. My other hand supported her back slightly below her neck as she curled in agony with every push, each more overwhelming than the last. Two more midwives joined us and crowded in to place a stethoscope onto Mira's belly, checking the baby's heart rate after every contraction. After what felt like an eternity, it seemed like no progress had been made. Mira gasped for air. Her eyes scanned the room with the expression of a lost child desperately searching for relief. I whispered encouragingly, "You got this, Babe."

In all the research Mira and I had done, the books we read, the classes we took, the advice we received, one piece of information managed to elude us. We learned about the back pain and the timing between contractions. We learned about the stages of cervix dilation and even about delivering the placenta after the birth. What we failed to consider and what no one happened to mention, was how long it took to push a baby out of a body, the final stage of giving birth. "Don't worry, on average it only takes around two hours," the midwife said, trying to assure us. When I turned to Mira, her bewildered expression conveyed simply, *"What? No. I'm done. I can't do this anymore. Help me."*

"Breathe." I gave her as reassuring an expression as I could muster, even though I found it impossible to fathom how Mira—how anyone—was capable of enduring the intensity, the frequency, and the duration of this pain. Sitting there holding Mira in my arms, advice from my mother echoed in my head. "Just when you're ready to give up, she'll be born."

Mira began to push again and the purple crown of the baby's head began to emerge. My eyes teared. I turned to Mira who was revelling in the few seconds between contractions. The oscillation between the painful pushing followed by seconds of relief continued for another hour and a half. Finally, a particularly forceful push thrust the baby out as if it was the end of a waterslide. The baby launched into the midwife's arms who, in a fraction of a second, placed her on Mira's chest. When I looked to Mira, her face expressed shock. Her eyes turned to me.

"It's a baby," she cried, astonished in what she'd done.

"It's a baby." Tears rolled down my face. "Baby Vivian."

"Vivian," Mira whispered with a smile. I overheard the kind giggling from the midwives, who asked if I wanted to cut the umbilical cord. With a childlike grin, I accepted without speaking. I took the scissors and cut the cord.

As I watched my daughter open her eyes, innocently discovering the new world around her, a sense of relief came over me. Not only was Vivian born healthy, but in her I found purpose beyond any I could ever contrive. I now had a being who relied on me to keep her safe, happy, and healthy. If ever I found myself in the depths of my own despair, I could now focus on why I needed to heal and work to accomplish it. What's more was the gratitude I felt. The motivation to raise Vivian superseded any other force to get better. Further, I could no longer face my demons by selfishly tormenting the ones around me. I framed healing on my own to be empowering, not daunting. I vowed to find the tools and do the work that would help me accomplish this task.

A piece of advice I'd heard was that the best way to be

a father to a child is to love the baby's mother. Mira and I had endured individual as well as collective challenges. Fortunately, surviving them drew us closer. We had gone from each other's enabler to each other's cheerleader. We were better equipped for our new journey as parents.

Repression

THE SCIENCE AROUND REPRESSED MEMORY IS INCONCLU-
sive. A tidal wave of reported cases of recovered
memories in the 1980s polarized groups of psychoana-
lysts, culminating into what was known as the "memory
wars." There were implications that therapists knowingly
or unknowingly influenced their patients into believing
abuse occurred. Meanwhile, the US justice system went
so far as to amend the statute of limitations for child
abuse from fifteen years after the abuse to three years
from the date the memory was claimed to have been
recovered. While the debate is ongoing, neither side dis-
putes the fact that childhood sexual abuse is prevalent
and tragically, shockingly commonplace.

I'm not advocating for either side of the memory wars.
I don't believe it to be the extraordinary phenomenon
that some imply it is. In my case, my conscious mind did
not bury the memory of the rape to the point of amnesia.
Rather, my subconscious decided instead to *distract* my

conscious mind until I was ready. Perhaps my point is semantic, but I maintained a constant state of distraction for almost forty years: acting out as a child, common for most children thus unrecognizable as a sign of inner turmoil; withdrawing within to play alone for countless hours; ultra-marathons of television, movies, music piercing my eardrums from my Walkman knock-offs; working to the point of isolation; bucket lists under the guise of life experience; social media, porn and, finally, drugs and alcohol. Our culture has made it abundantly easy to not look at oneself.

However, lurking like a man-eating shark in shallow water, I knew something was wrong and I knew that the dark silhouette of Spiderman had something to do with it. I knew something happened in my room that night, and I knew what. It lived in my periphery like trees we pass on a train and I dared not look at it directly. And because I didn't look closer, the boy, the teenager, and the young adult lived tormented, confused, angry, and depressed lives. The fear, depression, awkward sex, and painful relationships all reminded me something was wrong. Still, I dared not peek.

What's more, I tormented everyone I let in my life. I stung each of them with one small, hurtful act after another. It was like a Chinese water torture, driving them—and myself—a little more insane one drop at a time. With Gianna, Perrine, and the others, I broke down crying as I lay beside them while they held me. When they asked me what was wrong, I had no answer. Mira took the brunt of my decline when she became a part of the worse before the better. And she did it as she dealt with her own demons. Thankfully, gratefully, she is also a part of the better.

I'd be remiss if I presented everything in my life as agony. There were many meaningful, positive moments. The statement of encouragement from Uncle Garry, public praise from my high school English teacher Mrs. McKinnon, the kindness of friends along my journey. My father who woke up in the middle of the night to my screams to sit with me and assure me that Bigfoot didn't really exist. And Mom, who reminded me that I was loved every day and later patiently, painfully helped me avoid prison. I wasn't alone my entire life. I was alone in my pain without the ability or confidence to articulate it.

* * *

Given the legal prohibition, there have been no studies about the long-term effects of MDMA, but its use is promising as seen in the 2019 documentary *Trip of Compassion*. Personally, I loved the drug and the ability to bounce back after a weekend of a couple of pills, if I managed to keep it at that. But to continually take them every few days over the course of years unsurprisingly took its toll. I could not identify, with any degree of certainty, whether an emotion I was feeling was real. I physiologically lost the ability to be happy and to love as my body relied on the drug to provide the manufactured version. I forfeited my self-confidence and ability to think logically at work, while my short-term memory became a snowy, out of tune television channel. I was unceasingly exhausted, leaving no energy to exercise, and I settled for junk food which only exacerbated my health decline. It was a perfect storm for accomplishing the task of dying a painfully slow death, while yearning for a quick one.

To be clear, I take full responsibility and do not blame the drugs. The drugs were only a tool to help spiral me down to the bottom rungs of my own personal hell. But they also helped open my mind and getting me straight. The panic I suffered when facing what lurked in the depths of the "bad" mushroom trip, followed by the agonizing weeks and months it haunted me, have become a revelation for which I am deeply grateful. I was given the epiphany that my life was in my hands, and for the first time in forty-some years I could see myself for who I really was. No masks, no fake personas. No successful entrepreneur, no philanthropist, no endearing son. No loving brother, no loyal friend, no supportive husband. Just me, the man who was hurting people and himself.

Friendships forged in the years of my decline were genuine, intense, inspired and, like all things, fleeting and unmaintainable. We were lost together, bonded by our drug-empowered codependence. We acted as though we endured tremendous adversity together, when all we really did was indulge ourselves to the point of depravity. We harnessed exhaustion to mask the overwhelming reality of our respective lives. We were at each other's side through the darkness, and if one of us made it to the light, the bond severed. I will forever cherish those dark flights tethered to my lost compatriots. I owe them endless gratitude for the precious moments we danced under the electric sky. I wish them all the joy that life brings, and hope one day we can find each other on the other side.

Loving-Kindness

EVEN THOUGH MY LIFE SEEMED TO BE ON THE RIGHT track, there was much more work to be done, and I know that this will always be true. Meditation, one of the most powerful practices in changing my life, provided solace rather than escape, and I wanted to learn more. In seeking new techniques, I found one that served more as therapy than a breathing practice. Metta, or Loving-Kindness, meditation is the act of sincerely sending positive thoughts and well wishes to other people and to yourself. I listened to a guided meditation by Sharon Salzberg to help me through my first attempt. The exercise began with wishing four positive messages to myself by repeating a few phrases. The Salzberg meditation uses the following: *May I be safe. May I be happy. May I be healthy. May I live with ease.* Taking relaxing breaths, I focused on each. Characteristically, my mind jumped into how-can-I-do-this-better or how-do-I-fix-it mode.

May I be safe. I'd like to be safe. Am I being safe? How

can I keep myself safe while still enjoying life? I can take things slow. Relax, Rob. You're being safe.

May I be happy. Shit, that's a big one. Where do I start? Meditation says I start now. I can do that. I can choose to be happy now. I'm relaxed, I'm learning something new, I'm happy about that. Wait. Is that the point? Can I always relax, breathe, and decide to be happy? Maybe there's something to this.

May I be healthy. I can be healthy. I'm already on a roll. I can eat better. I can exercise more. I'm going to do that. A little bit more every day.

May I live with ease. Salzberg defines "lives with ease" as our ability to live without too much anxiety. I can work on this. Confrontations with family or coworkers cause me the most anxiety. Just the thought of a ten-minute phone call with my father flips my stomach in the wrong way. Okay, I can avoid confrontation by being better prepared and entering into potential conflicts mindfully and respectfully. If I get too agitated, I can breathe or step out of the room and take a minute. As for Dad, I made the decision that I want him to be a part of Vivian's life and Vivian a part of his, so I'll go into those calls or visits with compassion and patience. I also want to set a positive example for Vivian.

Next, I was to picture someone I love and hold their image and presence in my mind while repeating the same wishes. I pictured Mom. I know she's worried about me and her retirement. I want to wish her well. May you be safe. May you be happy. May you be healthy. May you live with ease. My eyes still shut, I felt my mouth form a smile. It felt good to send my Mom positive thoughts.

After a few minutes I moved onto the next subject for my well wishes, a perfect stranger. Someone I may only ever come in contact with once or twice. A grocery store clerk, a delivery man, someone at the office I'd never communicated with other than to give a passive half-smile as we passed each other. I pictured a neighbour, an old man wearing a turban who walked passed my house every day on his morning walk. May you be safe. May you be happy. May you be healthy. May you live with ease. Once again, I smiled.

My body felt warm, relaxed with positive thoughts. I felt contented not only with the practice of wishing people well, but that I was learning, that I was bettering myself and my life. The final specific individual to receive my directed rumination was a person with whom I have difficulty. Someone I may consider an enemy, or even hate. *What. The. Fuck. Okay, I can do this. Who do I have trouble with? There's that guy at work. Shit, there's Dad. Well if I'm going to do this, I'm going to do this. Who do I hate? What about the guys who bullied me in high school? I should probably work on letting that go? I can do this.* Dad, may you be safe. May you be happy. May you be healthy. May you live with ease. Just then Salzberg said, "If you find that this is too difficult for you, you can focus back on wishing yourself the positive thoughts, as you are now the one who is suffering." *I'm okay. I don't need to focus on myself. It feels good to wish my dad, someone I know, to be a good human, to wish him positive thoughts.*

As I sat alone on my sofa a few weeks into daily Loving-Kindness meditations, the contentment evaporated. My body and mind sat catatonic. I'd only ever thought about the man who raped me as a memory, an apparition. I'd never thought of him as a human being. *Fuck that guy. He doesn't deserve anything but torture and death. What if he raped others? Fuck him. Fuck him. Fuck him!* Instead of ending the meditation immediately, I turned to the one Salzberg provided and wished good things for myself, the one who was now suffering. *May I be safe. May I be happy. May I be healthy. May I live with ease.* Tears ran down my cheeks as I repeated the mantra long after the guided meditation was over.

It was clear to me that I hadn't yet confronted, or even acknowledged, my feelings about the rape. I reassured the eight-year-old boy in my letters to him in therapy. I quelled and forgave the angry teenager. I made peace with the adult who was so very lost for so very long. But I hadn't yet enveloped the negativity of my life to let it go. Not to "get over it" or "deal with it." I don't believe these memories will ever go away, nor is it something that people simply "get over." Rather, I needed a better way to frame it all and let go of my attachment to it.

I recognized that whatever had transpired in my life made me what I am today, which is a loving husband, father, friend, and human. I decided to accept that my rapist was suffering. I prayed he hadn't raped anyone else, and I hoped he was able to heal himself, even find peace. I spent months trying to wish him well, unable to even think the phrases. When I finally could, I was unable to be sincere. After what may have been thousands of attempts, I broke through. I sat on my basement floor on a small meditation pillow gifted to me from Mira's parents and I cried. *May he be safe. May he be happy. May he be healthy. May he live with ease.* I no longer harbour any anger or ill will toward the man who raped me. I forgave him and when I did, the anger, the sadness, the excuses for not living an honest, even happy life, dissolved into the ether.

To dig into the science a little, I found study after study concluding that Loving-Kindness meditation decreases migraines, chronic pain, PTSD, even schizophrenia-Spectrum Disorders. The practice activates empathy and emotional processing in the brain, increases gray matter volume, compassion, empathy, and self-love through curbing self-criticism. I wasn't alone in realizing the benefits from the practice. I still practice it today. The challenge now has become to find anyone I encounter that I have trouble with. I have no more enemies.

Sustaining Joy

THE DEEP DEPRESSION OF LAYING AROUND DIZZY FROM
drugs is now replaced with joy, fulfillment, and purpose
as I savour every second of my baby discovering her surroundings. Like any father, I wanted to be the best I could
be. I read parenting books voraciously, but I needed more.
Books I read on spirituality were profound with every new
revelation, but I sought an ethical framework on which I
could be a true role model. My healthy disillusionment
with organized religion made this challenging. I'd long
said goodbye to the dogmatic ideology of Catholicism
and, with it, other Abrahamic religions. What I searched
for covered a wide spectrum with everything from the
ethics of day-to-day life to the answers to, or at least plau-
sible theories pertaining to, life's big questions.

After reading Ryan Holiday's *Ego is the Enemy* and
The Obstacle is the Way, profound in and of themselves, I
dove into the Stoics like Marcus Aurelius and Seneca. I
studied every Eckhart Tolle writing and talk I could find.

I listened to the Rich Roll Podcast which consistently encouraged and empowered its listeners to live their true authentic selves. The book *10% Happier,* by Dan Harris, comforted me because here was someone who, like me, had been lost in Ecstasy and found his way back to help other people. Harris's book begot Sharon Salzberg ,whose books I devoured and still reread to this day. *The Book of Joy,* by His Holiness the Dalai Lama and Desmond Tutu, and Thich Nhat Hanh's *Living Buddha, Living Christ* drew me closer to a spiritual discovery exempt of any strict dogmatic prerequisite. It took decades for me to realize the lessons that resonated with me the most were from Buddhism.

Buddha said he wasn't a god and that we all have an immutable, perfect being inside us called our inner Buddha Nature. No matter how badly we screw up, we can always turn our lives around and, with work, even achieve enlightenment. The thought of having my own Buddha Nature not only gave me confidence, it held me accountable for my actions. If I wasn't being kind, I was hurting myself. I had myself to encourage, to empower. Whenever I screwed up, be it in life or in meditation, the next breath I could correct and be back on a better path. As for enlightenment, it doesn't have to be a magical place where someone becomes omnipotent. It can simply mean being a better human in this life. If the enlightenment some Buddhists describe is real, what a wonderful surprise. Also, in Buddhism any beliefs around phenomena that cannot be explained scientifically can be held as a maybe. If you want to suspend your belief about rebirth, that's fine; just be kind to all beings, which includes yourself. Not sure about karma? Okay, just be kind to all beings. Not sure if there even was a man who found enlightenment? Cool, just be kind to all beings.

Buddhists live under a set of rules known as Five Moral Precepts. These are: to not harm any sentient beings including yourself; to not lie or gossip; to take only what is freely given; not to take intoxicants; and not to engage in sexual misconduct (don't cheat on your spouse or mess with someone else's spouse). These ideals are what I choose to live by.

I *walk* different, slower, as a Buddhist. I breathe mindfully, taking in as much as I can around me. My life, however, is still filled with reminders of my years of decline. An innocent capsule filled with turmeric on my kitchen counter whispers to me to empty the spice to replace it with Molly. A palm-sized plastic bag filled with a microfiber towel in my sunglasses case makes me wonder how many capsules will fit inside. These thoughts recall the memory of how I used to live, and with it a head-shaking grin before I let them go.

I made a decision when I asked Mira to marry me. This is to be read slowly: I-made-a-decision to let go of the pain of the past and resign myself from the worries of the future. I vowed to love deeply and vulnerably without reservation or defense. I show gratitude every day, in writing. If I feel insecure or jealous, I strive to be thoughtful and transparent. I made a decision to make Mira a part of the centre of my life, alongside myself. I made a decision to be honest even if my voice shakes. I made a decision about how I want to think and how to act when no one is watching.

The joy I find in every day of my life didn't come overnight. It was not one thing. There is no secret. It wasn't the birth of Vivian, or a revelation during a mushroom trip, or the discovery of meditation and gratitude, or the clear water in Walden Pond. It wasn't the realization that I had ostracized all the people I cared about, or what it was doing to my family, or even my declining health. It was all of it. It was something in me that unyieldingly pushed in the right direction. It was accepting and owning that my life was moving one step forward and five steps back, then desperately jostling my way to one step forward and four steps back. Inching forward again until there were more steps forward than steps back. I refuse to dishonour any momentum I achieved, no matter how many steps I had fallen. No matter how minute the victory of a single step forward was, it served as motivation to press on.

Red Ink

DESPITE ALL THE EPIPHANIES, THE JOY, THE AMAZING wife and perfect daughter, the pain hasn't disappeared. Problems still persist. Sex is still awkward at times and my ability, and willingness, to initiate sex is barely existent. I wish I could say my wife has endless patience and compassion, but she's human like the rest of us with wants, desires, and insecurities. There is also the question of fatherhood. I aspire to be a positive, calm, happy father who fosters a strong confident empathetic woman, but I struggle to reconcile the fact that I've caught a glimpse of the worst humanity has to offer. I feel I have to navigate Vivian through a painfully narrow maze on a moving path in a field of hell, not unlike a hallway in a crowded prison where pedophiles, murderers, rapists are reaching for her. Who can I trust? How can I trust? I still suffer from visions and memories of the distant and not so distant past, causing me to wince in embarrassment and shake my head. I make amends where I can, but mostly I let it go. Anne has since retired, but I have found a new therapist with whom I am working to overcome these issues. Kevin is still around, but he keeps to himself.

Throughout my personal journey, my company continued to grow but it required more than full-time attention. I woke up at 4:30 a.m. for my morning routine, and was able to spend a few minutes with Vivian before leaving for the office. On nights when I was lucky, I spent a few minutes more with her. Mira texted me videos of Vivian's progress as she lifted her head for the first time or tasted a new food. The videos were bittersweet. I started to do the math. If I were to sell some more of my owner-ship, could I leave the company I started with Mitchel and Jordan? I ran and reran the numbers, each time asking myself what I really needed, each time re-evaluating what was truly important to me. With some sacrifice and a modest lifestyle, I could retire. When I asked myself how much more money I would make in the next few years if I didn't sell, and how much of that money I'd give up to spend those years at home as a father, the answer was clear: All of it. If I retired now, we might have less stuff, but we'd have so much more.

I approached Aaron and my work colleagues who were all supportive. Not too long after my decision, we closed a third round of investment financing which pro-vided me an opportunity to sell. At a final "all hands" meeting, which now included hundreds of staff, Aaron surprised me with a dedication. His kind words brought tears to my eyes, and I was able to address the company to explain my departure and wish them well. I was now free to be a full-time father and husband, and to embark on a lifelong dream. The Monday following my retirement, Vivian crawled for the first time. I was by her side.

Mira and I agreed our new financial position required us to live a simpler life. We sold the house. As we purged most of our belongings, I came across a discoloured, delipidated banker's box. It looked like a familiar old shoe I hadn't worn in decades. The type of shoe that wasn't really useful anymore, but throwing it away may result in losing the memories you and the shoe shared. When I opened the box, I took in the aroma of my teenage years. A mix of mold and dry wood. A mess of stained sheets of paper with black type under Pollock-esque slashings of red markings half-filled the container. Under the paper sat green and black notebooks yellowed from the years. My throat forced a gulp down to my stomach, which now filled with fluttering butterflies. The crate held inside it all the creative work I'd written as I was a teenager—the short stories I wrote in the years I was grounded living with my father, and the writing journals where I violently scribbled ideas, characters, and dialogue. The box held the dreams of a confused and lonely teenage boy. The dreams of becoming a writer.

The red ink on the printed pages was how I edited my work in a world without laptops. I spent countless hours printing and red-penning the passages I believed I could improve. The collection, complete with red ink, was now a memento inviting nostalgic reverence of work so poorly written. Putting my purge on pause, I began to read.

The first short story was about a boy who was witnessing a boy bullying another boy in the school washroom and stepped in, sacrificing himself to protect the victim. The two became fast friends, but there was no resolution to the bullying. The next story was about another boy being beaten by his peers at school, and wishing he'd become a vampire to exact revenge. The boy's wish came true but when an opportunity presented itself, he chose not to continue the cycle of violence. When I opened the notebook marked "Big book of ideas," I found a dozen more stories about unexplained violent behaviour. I stepped back into the hurt, confused teenager who wrote them. I took a deep breath as a dialogue played out in my head.

"I'm sorry you're going through this, man, but it's going to be okay."

"Really? Because this part sucks. I'm always alone. I don't think I'm going to make it."

"You're going to make it and it will get better. I promise!"

"Thanks, I guess. What makes it better?"

"We're surrounded by people we love and who love us. We also have a beautiful daughter! Hang in there because it's worth it."

"I'll try. Are we a real writer?" The question stumped me.

"Not yet, but I think it's time."

Disclaimer

THIS BOOK IS A MEMOIR AND I'VE DONE THE BEST I CAN to tell the stories as they happened to the best of my recollection. That said, some of these memories are old and I was high for many of them. I've asked people who were there but they were high too; still most agreed to their correctness. For painfully obvious reasons, some names and identifying characteristics were changed to protect the privacy of those depicted, not that any of them talk to me anymore. And dialogue has been recreated from the best of my recollection, but some exchanges are composites of more than one interaction. As for chronology, I have Expedia, Visa, and my bank account statements to thank for keeping me on track, but a few events may have been composited and/or reordered for the sake of story cohesion.